Craigroyston Days

*This book is dedicated to
the staff and students of Craigroyston,
1972–93*

Craigroyston Days

The Story of an
Educational Revolution

Hugh MacKenzie

MAINSTREAM
PUBLISHING

EDINBURGH AND LONDON

First published in Great Britain in 1995 by
MAINSTREAM PUBLISHING COMPANY
(EDINBURGH) LTD
7 Albany Street
Edinburgh EH1 3UG

ISBN 1 85158 706 3

A catalogue record for this book is available from the British
Library

Subsidised by THE SCOTTISH ARTS COUNCIL

The publisher gratefully acknowledges the support of Lothian
Regional Council and the Bernard van Leer Foundation in
the production of this book

Phototypeset in Caslon 3 by Intype, London

Printed and bound in Great Britain by
Butler & Tanner Ltd, Frome, Somerset

Contents

Acknowledgments

Thanks to Kirsty, my daughter, for planting the seed that became this book and her continual prompting to make sure it actually happened. Thanks to my wife, Joyce, for being an understanding and encouraging first-line editor, sounding-board, memory bank, and the supplier of cool drinks as I struggled with the book under the carob tree in Spain.

It would have been totally out of character for a book about Craigroyston not to have the assistance of past and present staff and students. No praise is too great for Margaret Hubbard for her thoughtful editing, encouragement and the time she made available to me. Also, thanks for her gift of the Ladybird guide-book *The Writing of Memoirs*. It actually worked! Thanks to Rab Purves for his preliminary work on the cover and to his ex-colleague, Maldwyn Stride, for his professional advice on the photographs. Thanks to Alan Munro, his sister, Joanna, and Pat Coburn for helping a computer illiterate

7

to complete the word-processing tasks required to meet the deadlines.

Thanks to the various research efforts of Jean Mackenzie, Pam Aitchison, Pat Coburn, Hwyell Williams and a special thanks to Wallace Wood, who kept the archive material for the school for over 20 years. Thanks to Luis de la Cuadra (alias Lewis MacStables) for helping with the photocopying.

Finally, thanks to Lothian Region and the Bernard van Leer Foundation for their generous sponsorship, without which this book would not have been possible.

Foreword

During every period of Scottish education, there emerges a headteacher who is unique; an individual who is significantly different from nearly all other heads. This very difference can lead to a period of change, where, by successful example, new management practices and attitudes are followed and schools improved. Hugh MacKenzie was one such head.

It must be remembered that Hugh MacKenzie became headteacher at Craigroyston High School in 1972. Most heads then were traditional in their views, often cautious about educational change, preferring to be known as excellent administrators and organisers, and of course firm disciplinarians, but, in the main, they did not welcome curriculum development and other changes. Not so Hugh.

From day one at Craigroyston, Hugh MacKenzie made it clear to all that the school belonged to the young people of West Pilton, to the 'students' as they were known. To move the attitudes of staff and successfully achieve this ethos, Hugh required a will and a determination not often seen in school managers of that time. But succeed he did, and Craigroyston became a very early model of a 'child-centred' state school.

Not surprisingly, at every possible opportunity Hugh MacKenzie attracted staff of the highest calibre who were equally committed to his philosophy – providing the right education for the children of West Pilton. I remember well, in my early days as the director responsible for staffing, interviewing teachers from all over Lothian Region and elsewhere for promoted posts in Craigroyston. In almost all cases, those appointed were not only seeking promotion but were attracted to the growing reputation of the school generated by Hugh MacKenzie's management style and educational views. It did not take too long before there was cohesion in the staff, with declared common aims and educational objectives.

There were many examples of notable changes in curricular thinking which came out of Craigroyston and spread throughout Lothian and Scotland. The creation of a team of staff committed to outdoor education and de-schooling was led personally by Hugh. However, the most striking example of all was the construction of CSE courses and awards, all seen as having particular relevance to the students, even though this meant an input from south of the border. This bold move by Hugh MacKenzie was soon followed by large numbers of headteachers throughout the country.

Not surprisingly, Hugh and his staff had a fair share of pupils who needed special care and attention. Here, too, innovative thinking took place, and to my knowledge the first ever 'school house' was created, which over the years kept a large number of young people in mainstream schooling who otherwise would have been permanently excluded. Craigroyston under the headship of Hugh MacKenzie was the first school to put into practice the earliest work on what has become Lothian's much-vaunted Youth Strategy policy.

It was early in 1973 that I first heard the term 'community school', when Hugh shared with me the drafting of a letter to the director, expressing his vision of Craigroyston for the future. In many ways it took too long to achieve that goal, but achieve it he did when the school's work was recognised by the Education Committee and Craigroyston was officially designated a community school in 1985. Without doubt, Hugh and his colleagues worked way beyond the norm to achieve this status, which was magnificently resourced by the Bernard van Leer Foundation and significantly supported by Lothian Region.

Those of us who know Hugh MacKenzie best know him to be a complex man, capable of very strong emotions. Over the years it became evident that Hugh needed surges of his own adrenaline, which, again and again, would push him and the school he cared for so much on to new ground. This push stayed with him, with such projects as 'Craigie Goes to Europe', until the day he decided to retire.

Appointed by Edinburgh Corporation, Hugh MacKenzie became one of Lothian's outstanding head-teachers – and no doubt would have been a success in any chosen field. I have written this contribution with great pleasure because Hugh made me feel a part of Craigie too!

All teachers will enjoy reading this book. It deserves

to become compulsory reading for all students who would be teachers.

Fraser Henderson
Deputy Director of Education
Lothian Regional Council

Prologue

One afternoon during the October holiday of 1971, I was in the garden of our family home in Edinburgh playing with the children when my wife, Joyce, called from the house to say that there was a telephone call from Educational Headquarters concerning an interview for a headteacher post. I thought it must be a mistake. Although I had applied for posts at Craigroyston Junior Secondary School, Niddrie Marischal Junior Secondary School and Darroch Junior Secondary School, I had been told the previous week that I was considered too young to be a headteacher and would therefore not be short-listed for any of the posts. My time would come, I was assured, possibly at one of the new community high schools currently at the planning stage in Edinburgh. However, the phone call was not an error. I had been selected for interview the following Thursday. With my age apparently against me, I concluded that my place on the short-leet was simply to make up numbers. For this reason, I felt little of the tension which surrounds inter-

13

views and looked on it as an experience that would no doubt stand me in good stead at a later date when I might reasonably expect to be promoted. This cavalier attitude convinced me that I should continue with my plans for the week's holiday programme, part of which was a round of golf at Gleneagles with three of my colleagues from Craigmount, where I was teaching at the time. This allowed very little time to prepare for the interview – as the underdog I could afford to be relaxed. The interview went extremely well, and the following day, when the telephone rang again, I was offered the headship of Craigroyston. I was overjoyed. Furthermore, I would not take up the post until the following session. I had eight months to prepare strategies that would turn a junior secondary into a child-centred school.

CHAPTER ONE

A Visit to the Clone Factory

In the summer of 1955, after completing my geography degree at Edinburgh University, I was working at Waverley Station as a porter, making some money before, reluctantly, doing my National Service in the RAF. When my call-up papers arrived, I found to my horror that I had been posted to the Army. Square-bashing was not what I had in mind so I set about finding a way to avoid it. I knew that studying at Moray House College of Education would give me a further year's exemption from National Service and a possible chance to re-apply to the RAF. Almost overnight, I became an enthusiastic trainee teacher, albeit for the wrong reasons. In the September I enrolled at Moray House, along with 20 out of 25 from the geography Honours class. This large number of prospective teachers did not reflect dedication to the profession, but rather the inadequacies of the University Careers Advice Service, which tended to send most Arts graduates to teacher-training college. A large percentage of the class were women opting for a profession in which, at that time, they were treated as second-class citizens – they could expect lack of equal pay, limited promotion prospects, and the expectation, if not at marriage, certainly at motherhood, that they would resign.

The function of Scottish teacher-training colleges was to produce recruits for Scotland's highly respected teaching profession. Moray House was a shock. After four years at university, the new graduates, accustomed to an atmosphere of intellectual and personal freedom, were suddenly thrust into one of control and enforced professional norms. In a sense, we were treated more as school-children than students. The college system – with its rules, dress code, and learning determined by a strict and compulsory-timetabled day, harnessed to fear of those in authority – was based on the techniques of schools.

The lecturers in charge of professional studies had four tasks. Firstly, they set about deflating our university background by continually explaining that our geographical knowledge would be of no use to us. In short, we knew nothing. Secondly, we were taught how to construct a standard geography lesson that could be used right across the subject and at all levels of academic ability. Thirdly, hours were taken up regaling us with stories, admittedly amusing, of student teachers' disasters on teaching practice. All of these tactics were confidence-reducing techniques; standard practice in the schools where the lecturers had their roots. Lastly, a great deal of time was dedicated to that major Scottish teaching resource, 'the tawse', a leather strap approximately two feet long, one end of which was split into three 'fingers'. With this primitive weapon children were punished. Hours were spent learning how to belt successfully, and in such a way that the pupils would always hold us in a combination of awe and fear. There was no discussion of the morality of corporal punishment. Rather, it was enshrined in that time-honoured statement, '*It never did me any harm.*' The discussion which took place was not on why, but on how. We were expected to conform to the use of corporal punishment but we needed advice on how to use the belt correctly: avoid marking the pupil's wrist; make sure you do not hit yourself on the follow-through. Dire warnings were issued as to our fate if we were not hard disciplinarians. The purchase of a Lochgelly Special was a primary expense.

The policy of pushing students to conform was emphasised by a series of lectures by the vice-principal to the male students and from the dean of women to the female students. For men, the blue suit, collar and tie, plus academic gown were *de rigueur*. For women, the skirt length and style, the blouse or the twin-set were considered weighty matters. Again, the lectures were marked by lack of discussion and an unshakeable expectation that the current dogma would remain unchallenged. Wearing academic dress and wielding the belt, we were launched into the schools as purveyors of knowledge, that key to success in the lad o' pairt's quest for professional status. My destiny seemed set. I would end up as one of the many blue-suited belting clones produced by the Scottish teacher-training system. At this point, fate threw in a rogue card.

CHAPTER TWO

A Subversive Mess

The tactic of delaying National Service and going to college worked perfectly. In August 1956 I was drafted into the RAF and in due course finished my training at RAF Jurby on the Isle of Man and became an education officer. Like all good jokes concerning service posting, I requested a tour of duty abroad and was posted to RAF White Waltham in Berkshire. It could be argued, of course, that in Scottish terms it was abroad!

Arriving at RAF White Waltham in December 1956, as station education officer, fate ordained that I met Flight Lieutenant Peter Drewitt, a command education officer. Although Peter was a regular career officer, he was a misfit. He was a man of the political left. This was a very unusual and highly volatile cocktail in an officers' mess, better known for its conformist right-wing attitudes. Peter had been influenced by his philosopher brother, Olaf, a former monk and Anglican priest, and through Olaf, Peter had studied the work of both A. S. Neill and Wilhelm Reich – two world-famous thinkers of

18

whom I had never heard. It was amazing to me that although Neill was Scottish, a world leader in the field of child-centred education, no mention had been made of him during my year at Moray House College of Education. In many ways this was not surprising, as he was certainly no blue-suited authoritarian. He had not followed the 'Gospel according to Moray House', although he had completed his original teacher training there. Many hours were spent in the mess with Peter discussing Neill and Reich – hardly the normal debating chamber for progressive education. He persuaded me to read A. S. Neill's *Hearts Not Heads in Schools* and *The Free Child*, as well as venturing into Reich's *The Mass Psychology of Fascism* and *Listen Little Man*. The latter was a fascinatingly simple book, explaining how, in Reich's view, mankind had the power to liberate itself into a more self-fulfilling world.

Neill's works also led me to the earlier pioneering child-centred educators Homer Lane and Bertrand Russell. Russell was a philosopher whose work I was particularly interested in exploring, as I had actually heard him speak at the original 'Ban the Bomb' meeting after the first Aldermaston March. All this intellectual stimulation led to a change in my attitude towards children, which in turn led to a shift in my thinking about the purpose and function of schools. I was gradually swinging away from the Scottish teachers' authoritarian system, based on the use of corporal punishment, to such an extent that I was continually involved in arguments with my fellow officers. Late one night after a mess dining-in night, I was arguing against corporal punishment with an air commodore who lost his temper and actually ordered me to bed. I had to leave the room but, as I did so, I thought how right Reich had been. The air commodore was, without doubt, one of Reich's armoured authoritarians. The consequences of this confrontation were made clear months later when the station adjutant, in his cups, told me that I had been investigated and my room searched for subversive literature. At this point the episode took on an element of farce, for in the meantime I had been made station security officer in charge of secret documents!

Increasingly, I questioned the values that had been inculcated at Moray House. Neill seemed so right and Moray House so wrong. The more I read and listened, the more sure I was, so that by the time I was de-mob happy in the summer of 1958 I was totally opposed to corporal punishment and thought that education had to be child centred. Committed to these two interesting but rather revolutionary ideas, I was very apprehensive about returning to Edinburgh and embarking on a career in the Scottish teaching profession.

CHAPTER THREE

The Liberators

Since Neill's philosophy is counter to the educational policies of the present government, it has been condemned once again to its former British oblivion. Apart from a few brief years in the late 1960s and early 1970s, Reich, Neill, Lane and Russell have never had any part, much less a significant part, in the training of teachers in Scotland. Many young teachers working in Scotland today have never heard of these men and their ideas. Others have only a sketchy idea. It is, therefore, necessary to go into some detail about Neillian education.

A.S. Neill was a man from my own nation who was kicking against the authoritarian nature of Scottish schools. He had been born in Forfar in 1883 and was educated in Kingsmuir Primary School by his father, the local dominie, or teacher. The Scots word *dominie* derives from the Latin word *dominus*, lord or master, and sums up the Scottish pupil-teacher relationship that Neill grew to abhor. His father conformed perfectly to the stereotype of the Scots dominie: the curriculum was academic and the authoritarian regime enforced by the 'tawse'. This early experience initiated Neill's life-long search for a completely different philosophy of education, where violence has no place and children are treated as children. He believed that children need to be allowed to be children in the process of growing up. This allows them to express themselves and builds their self-confidence. After teaching in various schools in Scotland, Neill became head of Gretna Public School in Dumfriesshire. At Gretna he found that he could not run the school in the child-centred way he wanted to because the School Board at the time would not permit his revolutionary ideas. The Board insisted that children have to be controlled, children must be beaten, children need to be forced to do everything. In direct opposition was a man saying children must be allowed to expand, children must be allowed to open out, children need to be children. Let children play, play, play, and then when they are ready they develop. This idea was so simple and so natural. It was the cornerstone of Neill's philosophy, and in Scotland in the 1920s it was dynamite. In time he founded Summerhill, a private school outside the state system, where he could put his ideas into practice.

Summerhill opened before the war in Lyme Regis on the south coast of England and then moved to its present site in Essex. Almost at once, Neill began writing about it. His books were translated into many languages, and very quickly he became a legend – but not in Scotland! Many of his ideas were developed from the philosophy of his friend Wilhelm Reich. Reich was a doctor and a psychologist working in Vienna and Berlin before the war. His School of Psychoanalysis extended the work of Freud, Jung and Adler. Reich was interested in liberating people through his radical ideas about sexuality. He believed that fulfilled and guiltless sexual expression is a liberating process. Reich was exploring ways of liberating people, and Neill saw education as a liberating process. This link drew them together, although Neill was acutely aware that he could not allow the children at Summerhill to behave in the totally natural way advocated by Wilhelm Reich. He knew that if he did that, if he allowed them to have sexual freedom and sexual expression, the authorities would close the school.

That was his only compromise. The rest of his child-centred philosophy he carried out. He encouraged play. Lessons were optional. He removed corporal punishment. It is important to reflect that the removal of corporal punishment was as revolutionary an idea then as lessons being optional would be today. Neill made a very important distinction between freedom and licence. The difference between them, he said, rested on responsibility. Freedom was a state of realising one's own potential in a responsible manner. Licence was mayhem. Quality education should lead children to learning that distinction for themselves. He set up structures whereby all the children were part of the decision-making process. The Government of Summerhill met regularly to determine policy and administer practice. Of course, with some children Neill failed – perhaps those who had been too badly damaged by the authoritarian system that they had previously rejected and which had rejected them. But Summerhill was a success. It produced many students who blossomed and developed despite the 'crazy' things they did at school.

Determined as I was to implement Neill's philosophy in my teaching, it is not difficult to understand my apprehension as I approached the Scottish system whose motto could so easily have been 'I tell't ye, I tell't ye. Keep *quiet* or I'll belt ye.'

CHAPTER FOUR

Back to Reality

Back in the 1950s there was a shortage of teachers, with the result that many unqualified people found jobs in the profession. Educational views were not important – the main question at an interview was about one's health. It was important that teachers attended regularly and did not put pressure on other staff who would have to cover the classes of sick colleagues. Having convinced the education authorities that I was healthy, I was appointed as a geography teacher at Niddrie Marischal Junior Secondary school, situated in one of Edinburgh's peripheral housing estates.

My first interview with the head and the principal teacher responsible for English, history and geography focused on the use of corporal punishment. The advice was simple – beat the children, both boys and girls, be strict and never show any doubt. 'Walk all over them!' was the maxim. Not an easy prospect when I intended to implement a child-centred philosophy and not use the belt at all. My determination not to belt was not only philosophical. I knew from experience that it simply did not work. I had been educated in a Scottish school where corporal punishment was the norm. Everyone lived in fear of the 'lash', wielded not just for bad behaviour but for not doing the work set or for doing it badly. One of the reasons I think I am not very good at languages is that I was belted every day in the French classroom, to the extent that a challenge developed between myself and the French teacher. Learning French became irrelevant. For me, the belt was the focal point in a power struggle.

In the violent environment of Niddrie Marischal it was not easy to avoid using the belt. Although teachers often romanticise about the wonderful days in junior secondaries, the truth is somewhat different. The pupils at junior secondaries were those who had failed the Qualifying Examination, a Scottish version of the 11-plus, at the end of primary school and entered secondary education seeing themselves as failures. The curriculum was not appropriate, and my memories are of time-fillers geared to keeping the pupils quiet. I remember walking along a corridor with a head of department telling me, 'The problem with working here is that I am wishing my life away. I just want every Monday-to-Friday stretch out of the road.'

I have to say I was struggling because I refused to belt the children, and the children took advantage of this. So it was, until one day the class wasn't doing very well, I wasn't doing very well, and the head came in and gave me a dressing down in front of the children. From that day on I had no further problem with discipline. The children saw me as being on their side and the head against me. In this strange way the children and I made contact, and it led to a remarkable breakthrough.

During this period, I joined the New Left Club in Edinburgh and became a member of the committee organising the annual programme. Having argued in favour of a series of lectures on progressive education, I was given the task of organising both the speakers and the events. It was quite easy to obtain agreement from Jack Stewart, head of Templehall Junior Secondary School in Fife, and R. F. MacKenzie, head of Braehead Junior Secondary School, also in Fife, progressives who were both, in different ways, challenging the model of the Scottish junior secondary school. R. F. MacKenzie was particularly scathing in his attack on the dead hand of the national exam system. I wanted to complete the programme by inviting Neill to take part. To my delight, he agreed. Lecturing and writing was the means by which he subsidised Summerhill.

As the time approached for his visit and it was agreed that Joyce and I would meet him, have a meal and take him to the University Staff Club where the meetings were held, I panicked. I thought, 'I don't want to meet him. I don't want to meet this man. I don't want to see the clay feet. I don't want to find anything wrong.' I was actually trembling when we met and there he was, in his corduroy suit and with his white hair, looking like the actor Findlay Currie. I made a comment to him, which I now can't remember, but it prompted him to respond, 'You've read Wilhelm Reich.' I knew I could relax.

The evening was wonderful. His lecture, in his own downbeat manner, was brilliant. He explained his philosophy that children need to be loved and not beaten, need

27

to be given space and time to play, need to grow up naturally. Given these conditions, and their corollary, the removal of fear, they will, in their own good time, turn to learning and blossom into balanced adults. He illustrated his points with a host of stories from Summerhill. He was crystal clear that he was describing freedom and not licence, a point which sadly many of his followers have not understood.

I have never forgotten that evening, listening to him and talking to him. I suppose that in modern terms it was like meeting a guru who did not let me down. His final comment to me when I told him that I wanted to move up through the state system and eventually run a Neillian school has stayed with me ever since. 'If you can do it inside the state system, then you are better than me. It will be very, very difficult.'

The headteacher at Niddrie Marischal, my first role model as a head, had served to emphasise my impression of Scottish education. The school was run by fear. I stayed there only two terms before I moved to Falkirk High School. At that time this was a traditional Scottish secondary school, which was, in many respects, the forerunner of the 1970s' comprehensive development. Here the rector was the pleasantly eccentric Chisholm Mackenzie, a man interested in children, taking their side in many of the problems which arose. Although he was liked as a person, the staff objected when he took the pupils' side. This antagonism made me very aware of the dangers a head faces if he strikes out on a tack completely at odds with most of the staff. He will produce an unworkable situation that will end in failure. There were already two examples of this, namely the headships of R.F. MacKenzie and Michael Duane. These heads, who were friends of Neill, were progressives and saw children as people to be nurtured, cared for and developed. Both saw the exam system as having the negative effect of perverting the educational process by driving the curriculum. Unfortunately, both men lost their staff in the struggle to put into practice a philosophy alien to British education. The books *The Unbowed Head* and *Risinghill: Death of a Comprehensive School* underline the tension among staff which, in both cases, resulted in a complete breakdown and in both men losing their jobs.

Falkirk High School was a senior secondary and I immediately built up an affinity with the academic lower end of each of the age-groups. Having just worked in a junior secondary, to me these particular children seemed very bright but to many of the staff they were academic failures. I built up a strong rapport with many of these children that pushed me in yet another direction. Every child is worth while. Every child has something to offer. Here was another facet of what Neill was saying that I was beginning really to understand.

After Falkirk I went to Broxburn Academy and then to Liberton High. Both of these schools emphasised the authoritarian approach, and the heads were remote, powerful figures. Both schools reflected two of the trends that belittled many of the young people of Scotland. Firstly, there was the desire to ape the private sector by introducing uniforms, prefect systems and complex school rules. These icons of establishment education clearly signalled to many young Scots that their own culture was inferior. Secondly, the Scottish tradition of academic excellence as the sole aim of education meant that a large portion of the school's population had their second-class status underlined on a daily basis.

In session 1968–69, while at Liberton, I was fortunate to win a place on an exchange programme to the USA. I spent a year at North Bethesda Junior High School in Montgomery County, Maryland. This was part of suburban Washington DC. Here I had the good fortune to work with Fred Cialli. As principal, he offered a completely different type of role model. Here was a head who was approachable and interested in new ideas. He routinely discussed education and led in-service training for staff. This was a new idea in education. As educational developments took place, staff had to keep up with these changes, and in-service training was, as the name suggests, training in the new developments for teachers already in the profession. The American experience showed me how schools could be run without uniforms, the student body casually dressed, and with a curriculum which was secular and, in many respects, comprehensive, albeit not in name. More importantly, the system ran without external exams. The teaching profession was expected to grade students without the expense and paraphernalia of a national examination system. This suggested that American society was prepared to trust its educators to carry out a professional task. The teachers were also confident in their approach to students. Praise and encouragement were the tools of the trade. This was in sharp contrast to Scottish education, where negative approaches dwelt on pupils' mistakes and weaknesses. Many educators criticised the American system as weak and lacking in control. This is not so. The top American students are as good as any in the world. Their system allows academics to progress. One of the contributory factors to this is that selection is delayed as long as possible, possibly right up to college level, whereas in Scotland the policy, at that time, was to separate the sheep from the goats as soon as possible and then concentrate on those of high academic ability. The Scottish way aptly illustrates the point made by Illich, the internationally renowned critic of our educational establishment, when he sees schooling as leading to teaching, and teaching therefore being a self-perpetuating profession.

Because North Bethesda Junior High School was situated in what was one of the most affluent and, consequently, most prestigious areas in the USA, I was exposed to ideas which had not yet crossed the Atlantic. The use of aims and objectives was a normal educational tool in the development of a curriculum appropriate to all levels of ability. The introduction of educational technology – televisions, computers, overhead projectors and photocopiers – to enrich the curriculum and change educational techniques was already in full swing. Here, I had my first contact with a resource centre, an extension of the library where students were trained in non-book-information-retrieval skills.

Part of the exchange programme was a series of visits to other Maryland and Washington schools. On one such visit I arrived at J. F. Kennedy High School, the jewel in the crown of the Montgomery County education system, whose assistant principal had the job of showing visitors round. He was obviously bored with this repetitive task and simply stated that the school was run on Neillian lines. I said I had met Neill. This electrified him, and over the school Tannoy it was announced, 'There is a man in the building who has met Neill.' Doors were opened for me, the red carpet was out and I saw a Neillian state school in operation. It wasn't purely Neillian –

it could not be in a state system. The children were not allowed to do as they wished, but it was Neillian in that it was not authoritarian. There were no rules, and the students were given room for self-expression. It was my first contact with an organisation inside the state system, albeit in another country, where people were saying, 'We are doing Neill.'

Not long after returning from America, I was appointed as deputy head to Bill Trotter at Edinburgh's new showpiece school, Craigmount. Bill was an excellent example of a thinking head. He was approachable and prepared to develop a broad-based curriculum. The deputy head of a Scottish school is often regarded as the school's disciplinarian. I made it clear to the staff that, while I accepted this role, I would not use the belt as a means of punishment. By this time I was adept at strategies for dealing with difficult pupils in my own classroom. As deputy head I had to learn how to handle discipline problems in other areas. This was vital preparation for becoming a non-belting head.

In my early years I had very occasionally used the belt, but 'revulsion' is not too strong a word to define my feelings about it. There is something wrong when an adult takes a leather strap to a child to make him or her do what he or she wants. At Craigmount I told the staff that I preferred them not to use the belt. I wanted corporal punishment de-escalated. Lines, detention and reasoning with the child were my preferred alternatives. Of course it was difficult when a member of staff brought to me a pupil who had refused the belt. I could not afford to alienate the staff, and I would not, myself, belt the pupil. The line I took was a compromise I was never happy with. I would try to persuade the child to take the punishment the teacher wished to mete out. When the belt was finally abolished in Scotland in 1987, I was delighted. Not only was the move close to my heart, but also my morally uncomfortable compromise was removed for ever.

The other significant aspect of my time at Craigmount was participating in the development of the guidance system. Bill Trotter was setting up a guidance structure in the school, and I was able to put my American experience to use and also implement Neill's philosophy. Having observed student councillors at work in North Bethesda High School, the way forward appeared to be to use the guidance staff as councillors who were both firm and fair. Discipline in North Bethesda was maintained not by an authoritarian structure but by talking out problems. My only criticism of this system was that the councillors did not teach, and this led to friction between the teaching staff and the guidance staff, i.e. the councillors. It was very easy for staff to turn on a councillor and say, 'You don't know what it is like in the classroom.' At Craigmount a guidance system was set up which worked well, although it is important to realise that the odds were in favour of it doing so, as the catchment area contained a cross-section of the socio-economic groups of west Edinburgh.

In October 1971 I found myself appointed head of Craigroyston Junior Secondary School with effect from the following August. My own education at the Royal High School of Edinburgh, my time at Moray House, the RAF, Neill, Reich, a range of Scottish secondary schools, and America all played their parts in forging my philosophy into a policy.

CHAPTER FIVE

The Making of a Heidie

Craigroyston, or Craigie as it was to become known, is situated in the north-west of Edinburgh on a council estate, most of which had been built since the Second World War when Edinburgh cleared its inner-city slums and rehoused the population in peripheral council estates. The houses were cheaply built because quantity was the priority in those post-war years. The suburb had some 20,000 people, but virtually none of the amenities one would expect to find in a town of that size. The most outstanding example was that there was no bank, although many attempts had been made, and were to be made, to persuade one of the Scottish banks to open up a branch in the area. At this time the population of the estate was young. The breakdown of the extended family caused by the rehousing of the inhabitants of the Victorian slums of central Edinburgh led to few older people moving into the peripheral housing area. This lack of an older stabilising population led to the problems which were to become characteristic of many such estates located in the major Scottish cities.

During the months I had to prepare for my move to Craigroyston, I spent a considerable amount of time finding out about the Muirhouse, Drylaw and West Pilton estates, part of the area which comprised the school's catchment area. The area was characterised by the socio-economic problems which beset all Scottish peripheral estates – petty crime, alcoholism, one-parent families, health problems, unemployment and poverty all existed in percentages far higher than the national norm. This was not the Festival City, but the Edinburgh bypassed by the tourists and known to other Edinburgh residents solely through the media's negative propaganda. All the makings of an urban ghetto were present. It was not long before the situation was exacerbated by the gradual decline in housing standards. Unpopular empty high-rise blocks and endemic rising damp in most houses produced a gradual drift of population to other parts of the city. This decline was compounded in the 1970s and 1980s by the scourge of drugs, the rise in crime necessary to feed that addiction and, later, the emergence of Aids.

The local population saw Craigie as an alien cultural institution to which they were forced to send their children, many of whom had learned that they were the failures of the Scottish system. Edinburgh is the most class-ridden city in Scotland, possibly in Britain, and the children of these areas knew that they were at the bottom of the heap. They saw themselves as failures and were treated as such. In most schools they were given a watered-down academic curriculum that was suited to neither their needs nor their abilities. The whole circus was held together by fear. Craigroyston had all the

35

hallmarks and stigmas of a junior secondary. At that time there was a six-layer structure in the city schools, and Craigroyston was firmly at the bottom.

When I tried to visit the school, the then administration made it clear that I was not welcome. This produced a major problem. How to find out about the school if I could not visit? What nonsense to suggest that I should turn up on Day One with no prior knowledge. I was lucky in one respect, in that some of the Craigroyston staff had worked with me in my Liberton days. Wallace Wood was head of the maths department, and from him it was possible to glean information which enabled me to work out strategies for the future.

I spent a great deal of time with subject advisers in order to find out in which direction each of the subjects was moving and what were the future trends. This gave me an insight into subject areas of which I knew very little and also allowed me to build up a positive relationship with the advisers, many of whom later became close and helpful colleagues.

The problem of visiting Craigie was solved by the then assistant director of education, Eric Ferguson. He simply pulled rank and took me to the school to meet the head. During the tour of the school it became clear what was deemed important – attendance and good time-keeping. Nothing about the curriculum or about the children.

At the end of the meeting I was told not to return until the following session, although an offer was made that I might meet the principal teachers, subject and guidance, if I felt I had anything of significance to discuss with them. However, the visit did allow me contact with Douglas Currie, who was to be the depute for the next

15 years. This was vital because it gave me access to the school's timetabler and enabled me to use the skills I had acquired at Craigmount to ensure that the sacred cow of the timetable was not used to block the changes I needed to implement.

Two personal contacts had pushed me in the direction of change. With my friend Harry Cohen, a lecturer in sociology at Moray House, I discussed how to approach changes in an institution. There are two possible ways. The first is to enter an institution, sit back and watch and, after some time, make the changes. The danger of this method is that the institution can become all-enveloping and then change becomes difficult. The gradualist approach is easier and consequently more acceptable to the staff.

The other solution is to go in and immediately introduce changes. The advantage of this is that the innovator does not become immersed in what people are used to. Weighing up these two approaches, I decided that the way forward was the second method. I took the view that I had not been appointed to maintain the status quo, but rather to lead Craigroyston in a new direction.

The second contact was made by pure chance. Life is full of these strange happenings. I was on a beach in Spain when I met Forsyth McGarrity reading a book. In time he became Her Majesty's senior chief inspector in Scotland, but when I met him he was a school inspector. At that time I was at Craigmount, and he was very interested in what I was trying to do.

For three or four summers I bumped into him in the same small Spanish fishing village. We used to chat about education, and he reinforced over and over again the crucial element of not losing the staff by moving too radically or too fast. By the time I was a head, attending head teachers' conferences, he was the chief HMI, and despite the pressure of his job, he always took an interest in my efforts to create a Neillian school.

I was well aware of the dangers. At Falkirk I had seen a head who had alienated the staff. I knew what had happened at Risinghill in London. There Michael Duane lost the staff and, as a result, lost his job. Although the final showdown at Summerhill Academy in Aberdeen was still two years away, the clouds were gathering. I could not risk making the mistake R. F. MacKenzie was making in Aberdeen. He had moved too quickly and lost the staff, forgetting that it was they who would be carrying out the work in the day-to-day contact with the students. *The Unbowed Head* is a study of the tension developing in the school, splitting the staff into factions which, in the end, resulted in the anti-MacKenzie faction destroying an interesting educational experiment. I knew progress could only be made by winning over a high percentage of the staff and, in particular, the principal teachers, who, as middle managers, are the controlling influence in a school. There was only one way forward – to walk backwards, asking people to follow me, not out in front running, because out in front if you turn around there may be nobody there.

I had to take the staff with me. One strategy I used was to appoint new teachers who were committed to child-centred education. As the spring term progressed, Eric Ferguson intervened on my behalf once again. He insisted that I was to be involved in the selection of all staff, whether probationer or promoted for the following session. This was a very interesting breakthrough which gave me a chance to select those I saw as like-minded.

There was a shortage of teaching staff in Scotland at that time, and many posts were filled by anybody who would take the job. Often, not too many questions were asked about qualifications. This situation existed at Craigroyston, and I hoped to change that when I invited a number of principal teachers to help interview prospective assistants. As products of the status quo, their main questions were still about health and attendance. Nevertheless, it was a step forward.

Three events conspired to help me with the appointments. First, it was decided to create a new post of assistant headteacher. All the applicants were internal. I was able to persuade the Education Committee to appoint Wallace Wood, whose support, for the duration of my headship, was invaluable. I relied on his meticulous attention to detail and grasp of the minutiae essential to the efficient administration of the Craigie curriculum. This freed me to develop Neill's philosophy and to devise strategies to implement it. The promotion of Wallace Wood left a vacancy in the maths department which was filled by one of the most committed maths teachers I have ever met, Jim MacDonald. At the same time, Eric Ferguson decided to split the science department into three disciplines, giving me the opportunity to appoint two new principal teachers.

The most important development in staffing was being able to appoint principal teachers. The PTs in a school have a very powerful position, in that they can control change, either restricting it or allowing it to take place. Eric Ferguson gave me all the help I needed to ensure that I had a group of colleagues at all levels, and crucially at PT level, who were loyal, hard-working companions and who wished to travel at least part of the road that I wished to travel.

The colleges at that time were beginning to produce more teachers, which meant that, for the first time, the school was fully staffed. During my last term at Craigmount I had access to Moray House students, and I persuaded many of them to accept a job at Craigie. Two of the other posts were filled in strange ways. I remember once phoning the parents of a prospective teacher, hoping to gain their support to persuade their offspring to work in Craigroyston. I knocked on doors trying to persuade good teachers I knew of that the school would be a worthwhile place to work. I once interviewed somebody in a pub!

I also had to win over the existing staff. I could achieve this by adopting the role of an enabler, a useful description often quoted about me over the years by Fraser Henderson, a current depute director of education. In the struggle to find a meaningful role, many headteachers resort to their own original skills based on excellence in the classroom. As head, I felt that the major task should be to reduce bureaucracy, protect staff from its worst effects, acknowledge their skill and try to make their jobs as rewarding as possible.

The staff also needed their confidence built up because of the position of junior secondaries in the structure of Scottish education. Edinburgh schools were a stratified hierarchy: public, independent, merchant company, former local authority fee paying, senior secondary and junior secondary. Over the years this has led to the apparently innocuous question. 'Which school did you go to?', the reply to which neatly placed the person answering in their correct niche in the city's society. The

Edinburgh Question exemplified all the values of the Athens of the North. It was imperative that the staff of this junior secondary school in north Edinburgh had its confidence built up to remove the feeling of being at the bottom of the pile.

I had to come up with curriculum packages to enable the staff to use their professional skills to promote better relationships with the students. After all, a school is an institution with an intelligent workforce, one which needs to be utilised, not stultified by the exam-led work it is required to do. At the morning break, before school and at lunchtime, I would be able to approach the staff in an informal way. In order to build the professional self-esteem of the staff, I intended to have an open-door policy, which meant that staff could come to my office at any time. Looking back, even this was unusual, but because such new management techniques soon became accepted, many schools later adopted these policies.

With help from the directorate, inspectorate and colleagues, my strategies gradually took shape. New appointments, winning over the existing staff, taking the pace slowly and revising the curriculum through control of the timetable – all of these were essential to delivering a Neillian child-centred education geared to the needs of the pupils without relying on fear.

The policies for Craigie's students became clearer. They needed confidence-building strategies. The young people in the catchment area had been told at the age of 11 that they were academic failures. The local media constantly referred to the area they lived in as a ghetto. The only news that emerged was negative and gave many young people an inferiority complex, which took the form of aggression towards authority. To have any hope of success, the confidence of the young people had to be built up and they had to believe they had something to offer society. The area they lived in might have faults. This was not a reflection on them, but on the society into which they had been born.

I thought one way of building the students' confidence might be to ask the staff to praise the children. This was a total reversal of the normal Scottish educational approach. Giving pupils tasks they could achieve and then encouraging them was, in my view, the way to build up self-respect. I also decided that once I became head I would contact the local and national press every time the school achieved something positive. This, too, would build the confidence of staff and pupils. Confidence-building strategies were pure Neill and, at that time in Scotland, radical.

The junior secondaries of Edinburgh locked themselves into a competition they could never win against the city's senior secondaries and private schools. They did this by aping the schools they regarded as the top layer, adopting many of their airs and graces to disguise their position. Pupils were forced to adopt the mores of the middle- and upper-class schools, and this placed them in direct conflict with their own background and produced many of the problems which led to their aggression towards authority. It seemed to me that to reduce the alienation I had to remove the trappings of these establishments. This could be done by getting rid of school uniforms, prize-givings and education built on competition, abolishing the prefectorial system, reducing rules and regulations, and producing a curriculum that reflected the needs of all, not just those who would go on to university. Lastly, it meant persuading staff to accept two further alien notions. I wanted them to hang up both their academic gowns and their belts. I knew that the former would be relatively easy. By the early 1970s academic dress was less common than it had been when I had begun my teaching career. The belt, however, I knew would be a powder keg.

To me, it seemed so clear, and yet when I compared what I was planning with my memories of Niddrie Marischal, it seemed Herculean. I feared being beaten in the same way as Michael Duane had been and Bob MacKenzie seemed to be heading towards. But there was no choice. This was the road I had been travelling since I had met Peter Drewitt 16 years before. I believed in Neillian education, and I was determined to make it work inside the state system. If I failed, like the other progressives, I would leave education. This I knew as surely as I knew that, no matter what the pressures, I would not run a school in the old way. I also knew that Day One would be the most important day of my professional life.

CHAPTER SIX

Day One – The Yellow Van Arrives

That Sunday evening in August 1972 I spent at Kilspindie Golf Club, trying to play with two long-standing friends. It was hopeless. Later on sleep was impossible. For months, Craigroyston had been in the future, but that night it was only a few hours away.

In the morning, I drove the family's yellow Dormobile to school, parked at the front door, walked in with my briefcase and made my way to the staffroom. The reaction was immediate. The staff were so unused to seeing the head in their room that one PT strolled over to tell me that I had an office along the corridor and offered to show me where it was. I said 'I know I have. It's okay, I am happy to sit here.'

The statement had been made. I was one of the staff, albeit with a different function. John Wells, one of the young staff I had appointed, came over, sat down and began to chat. I could hear the whispering – 'We can't have that. If he comes into the staffroom we can't talk about him.' They did not yet know that I hoped to build a different relationship with them. Sitting in the staffroom was a small step but a very significant one, illustrating the kind of relationship that I hoped to build.

We moved upstairs to the library, which had been set out for a staff meeting. At this point I made my second move, and at this people really did stare. I simply took off my jacket and threw it on to a chair. Unheard of! Very aware of the electric atmosphere, I opened my talk by saying that I had been appointed not to maintain the status quo but to make changes in the school. I told the staff I hoped, in the not too distant future, that Edinburgh's policies would convert the school into a sixth-form comprehensive. I intended to move it away from reflecting the standards and disciplines of the educated middle-class staff towards a curriculum which met the needs and aspirations of the young people living in the area. I had two immediate changes in mind. I wished to introduce a minority-time programme, an innovation which was beginning to gain momentum in Scotland. I would model it on the activity programme from Craigmount. 'We have tried all that before,' said a voice.

I replied, 'I know, but we are going to do it again, differently, and I am going to make it work.'

I explained that I wanted pupils to be known as students. This notion so shocked one of the PTs that he said 'As far as I am concerned, a bob is always a bob, Mr MacKenzie. I will call them pupils.'

'Fine!' Confrontation at that point would have spelled disaster.

We moved on to dress. There was still a dress code for staff at that time. Men wore suits; women wore blouses and skirts or dresses. Academic gowns sprinkled the room. I had made it clear, by the simple act of standing there in my shirt sleeves, that I had no intention of wearing a gown. I ventured a passing reference to the inappropriateness of academic gowns. There were no objections.

I then went on to say that the traditional restriction on female members of staff wearing trousers was out of step with the changing position of women in society. I intended to remove this anachronism. Women in Craigroyston would be free to wear trousers if they wished. The inevitable objection came – from one of the men. 'I disapprove of that. You are wrong. They shouldn't wear trousers.'

My response was, 'It is up to the ladies. It is nothing to do with you.' Risk! Confrontation! But I had the women on my side. Whether they wore trousers or not, for the first time they were being given responsibility for making their own decision.

As the meeting progressed, I was trying to win over group after group. After the clothing crisis passed, I turned to areas designed to address the younger staff, then the newly promoted staff, and even the traditionalists. It was carefully prepared, not too much, not too quickly, no commandment – thou shalt not belt. I went slowly, hoping that my strategy was working.

I explained that I was going to tamper with the school day by lengthening the morning break to 20 minutes and that I expected all members of staff to come to the staffroom at that time. The strategy was an attempt to break down individual cliques and create some degree of corporate unity. This might even lead to the revolutionary possibility that coffee and tea could be made for the staff, rather than the status quo in which everybody brought their own cup, tea, coffee, milk, sugar and Thermos flask! Interestingly, no one objected to the increase in the break time. Everybody agreed to use the staffroom, although a few did need reminding during the first few months.

I had hit upon the staffroom idea almost by chance. At the end of the previous term the Craigmount staff had been drawn against the Craigroyston staff in the annual Edinburgh staff golf competition. This had given me a chance to chat with people who did not know me, but who knew I was to be the head the following term. I found out that the staff very rarely met together and that they usually kept to their own parts of the building. They had seemed to welcome the idea of a central point where they would all meet.

The next area of contention was the use of the main staircase and the front door. The students were not allowed to use either. As far as I was concerned, the whole campus should be available to everyone. This was the first attempt to hand the school over to the students. I explained that I would not expect students to remain on campus during the morning breaks or lunchtime. The staff were ambivalent about this idea. It meant the end of duty rosters, but it also raised a definite query about my sanity.

In the past the children had had to walk on the left-hand side of the corridor. The staff stood at the doors; the children were lined up. The staff in effect policed the corridors. My policy was an attempt to change this. I wanted the staff to relax. I saw their job as being in the classroom with the children. No duty rosters would be put up for corridor patrol, lunch duty or lining up the children outside in the cold and wet. The students would come in to school for lessons and go off campus at break and lunch times if they so wished.

And so to the minibus! It was the next area of contention as it had previously been regarded as almost the private property of the technical department. Now it would be centralised, making it easier for other staff to make use of it. While this was not well received by the technical department, many other staff indicated that they would welcome easier access to transport.

Things were going well. I tried to speak to the staff as fellow human beings. I tried to let them understand what I wanted to do and how I saw my role in relation to them. While we were talking about outdoor education and de-schooling, I explained that I would make it easier. As an enabler, I was going to make it so. I wanted to remove the routine form-filling drudgery and make it simpler for the staff to deliver quality educational experiences to the students. That was part of my role. I wanted staff to use their initiative and to feel valued. I tried to convey the idea that I wanted to create an ethos alien to Scottish education. I wanted there to be an atmosphere which was friendly. I hesitate to use a word which has been so ill-used, but what I really wanted was a sort of love relationship – love in the sense of a caring between staff and students. I wanted staff to address me as Hugh, and I wanted them to understand I would never, intentionally, use the phrase 'my school'. As the years went on I frequently heard heads talking about 'my school', 'my English department', or 'my staff'. This is insulting. There is nothing possessive about it. As headteacher, I just had another function in the organisation. My role was to make the organisation work. Right from the beginning I stressed that I saw this as my primary role.

Gathering up my courage, I rounded off the meeting with a basic statement on corporal punishment. I would not use it. The result was a stony silence. I withdrew to my office. I had had to say it, but I did not know the effect it would have.

I remember walking down the stairs to the office, sitting down behind my desk and thinking, 'What do I do now? What do I do now?' It was terrifying. Heads have no training, no training whatsoever. I sat there thinking, 'What have I done? What's going to happen?' 'What does one do as a head?' I asked an empty room. Where does one go? There had been no real training for the tasks that lay ahead.

Eventually I went to a technical department meeting where the principal teacher was outlining a staff weekend at Lagganlia. He explained to me that in the past staff had spent occasional weekends at the city's outdoor centre. From time to time some of the more senior students also went along. I was interested that so many people in the room were keen to go to Lagganlia. At the end of the meeting I said I was pleased about this as it would be useful preparation for the entire third-year group spending five days in outdoor-education centres the following summer. It was my first opportunity to let the staff know about the huge drive into outdoor activities that I intended to pursue.

I knew one of the key areas was regular communication with staff. From my American experience, I was aware of the value of dialogue as a major technique in reducing rumours and staff tensions. The daily bulletin, an Americanism which had been successful at Craigmount, made its appearance immediately I started at Craigroyston. With its companion tool of pigeon-holes, the dissemination of information to staff speeded up. I deliberately did not have a pigeon-hole myself, in an effort to make it necessary for staff to talk directly to me during my daily visits to the staffroom. I was trying to make it clear that I was approachable. Both tactics seemed obvious methods of disseminating information, but at that time they were unusual.

Looking back on those early days, there was not a lot of open animosity. If people are used to an authoritarian head and his replacement comes in and starts by telling them what is going to happen, they accept it automatically. Teachers are trained to. There was no real challenge in the situation, although a vocal minority was trying to do just that. The hard belters told me they held the school together and assured me that it was going to be chaos. 'Everything will just disintegrate if you don't watch what you are doing,' they warned.

Against this, there were signs that some of the staff were willing to give me a chance. They liked the openness. Teachers are an educated, intelligent workforce. My experience as a teacher had been for the most part one in which the head of the school had treated the staff as being of little value, and I was determined not to place either myself or the Craigie staff in that situation. There was apprehension, perhaps even fear, but there was also a *frisson* of excitement and hope.

CHAPTER SEVEN

Hello, Students!

The next hurdle was the day the young people returned to school. The school assembly is another practice, copied from the private sector, which has, for generations, played an integral role in British schools. Assemblies have three functions. Firstly, they have a use in passing on information. Thereafter their existence is rather more ideological. They provide the element of religious education required by the state, and they inculcate a sense of corporate identity. Throughout my career, I had been conscious that the teachers at assemblies were present as surrogate warders, holding down the natural buoyancy of the young people in order that the platform party, normally the head, could conduct the business in hand. This was the practice I found *in situ* at Craigroyston. Daily assemblies were carried out in total silence, presided over by the head. A more potent symbol of authoritarian education would be hard to find. Discipline and power emanated from the head alone.

Previous practice required that I march on to the

platform and keep the students quiet for two or three minutes while information was read out, after which a quasi-religious service would take place. I was quite sure that I was not a lay preacher. Keeping the school quiet as an exhibition of power was not for me either. My antidote was to stroll down the passageway and, once on the platform, speak to the students in an informal manner. I wanted to establish a different kind of relationship between the staff and students.

During the first assembly it was vital to change the established tone, which many senior staff assumed would be continued. The imposed silence for its own sake was a non-starter. The casual approach seemed to work. I addressed the school as 'students', for the first time, and started the process of handing the school over to them. I explained that they could now use the front door and main staircase, leave the school grounds at morning break and lunchtime, or stay in the building as they wished.

This was placing the students in a position of trust, which was fundamental to the philosophy I wanted to develop. Naturally, there were incidents both in the local shops and the corridors, but if the students were never trusted they could not mature into responsible adults. This is a development too often lacking in the Scottish educational system.

I also asked that when I spoke to them in the corridors, the students told me their first name, but unfortunately this only happened once. I also stressed the importance of eye-to-eye contact when talking, and this did become a feature of Craigie students.

At the time I had no idea what effect this had on the student body, but, at Craigie's Silver Jubilee party in

1988, I had an interesting chat with two charming young women who had been present at that first assembly. They claimed to remember the casual clothes, the saunter through the hall and the friendly chat, although the details had evaporated with time.

I think this first assembly was when John Wayne first made his appearance. Like all good stories, the John Wayne nickname grew and was embellished over the years. Apparently, I always wore cowboy boots, but the truth is that I never owned a pair. One member of staff was having work done in her house. The carpenter was delighted to discover that she taught at Craigie and proceeded to regale her with stories about the cowboy boots and how I had once arrived at school on a horse which I had hitched to the front door!

Moving around Craigie filled much of my time in those first days. This made me a known figure, to both staff and students. Not being office bound was important to me. It gave me an insight into classroom teaching and, more importantly, contact with the students. I adopted a friendly role, speaking or just greeting students when we met. This approach also gave me an edge when students were sent to me for disciplining. They did not like it when the friendly approach vanished.

At Craigmount the various school houses had met for their own assemblies, and the head, if he needed to talk to any of them, would visit them in turn. This seemed to be an acceptable alternative, so I adopted this pattern. The whole school would be assembled only if and when the need arose.

One major assembly hurdle was still left. I had to be formally inaugurated as the head of the school by a councillor from the Education Committee. Eric

Ferguson contacted me to explain that I would be expected to assemble the school in the hall and introduce the councillor, who would then induct me as head. I was told to wear full academic dress. I refused and precipitated the first of many conflicts with the directorate. After several stormy telephone conversations with Eric Ferguson, he changed his position and supported me in the final argument with the director of education. As a result, when the platform party assembled in my office I was casually dressed.

Things did not progress to my liking. The councillor in charge of proceedings harangued me on the importance of aiming to send as many pupils as possible from Craigroyston to Oxbridge. To my horror, he addressed the school in the same manner. He harangued the students that their ultimate aim should be a university place at Oxford or Cambridge, and to effect this they should work hard. I avoided following up his remarks and instead talked to the students for two or three minutes about their school, their education and their future. If any students wished to go to university, they could do so perfectly satisfactorily in Scotland. I was at pains, also, to stress that there were many ways of being successful other than going to university.

I had insisted that afterwards the entire staff and not just the platform party would be invited to the library for coffee. All the staff were introduced to the director of education and the councillor. For many, this was the first time they had ever had any contact with the director.

CHAPTER EIGHT

Rules Create Crises

It is very easy for a head to make pronouncements and then retreat into the sanctuary of his or her office. In those days many staff had an image of the head picking up the *Scotsman* and spending all morning reading the paper and doing the crossword. This picture would not survive an open-door policy! I spent time moving about the school, rather than being identified with my office. Predictably, the policies I wanted to implement were creating tensions among the staff, and some of the cracks were beginning to appear. The new staff, who were mostly probationer teachers, were, in the main, supportive and keen to see policies which would make a significant difference to education and to their jobs. Most of the original staff had decided that I needed to be given a chance and were supportive in a distant way while reserving judgment. Naturally, there was a group which resented the passing of the previous regime and all that it stood for, and it was this group which produced most tension. The danger signals were there. Now was the time to remember that it was the teaching staff who would be implementing the changes.

Over the years, the teaching unions had been campaigning for a reduction in class size, in an effort to make education more meaningful and the teachers' task more rewarding. If a reduction in Craigie's class size could be achieved, more staff might accept the changes. Although Craigie was *de jure* a junior secondary, it was *de facto* a senior secondary. There was a minute number of fourth-, fifth- and sixth-year pupils who stayed on at Craigroyston. This meant tiny classes in the upper school. These classes had been skilfully added by the former regime. By rejigging these small senior classes and adding a three-teacher remedial department (one example of the support of the Education Department for a new head), it was possible to reduce the junior classes below the magic 30.

One small move that helped to win over the principal teachers was divulging the school finances and handing to the departments the power to purchase their own requirements. Previously the principal teachers had had to submit to the head their priorities for spending, and he had decided what would be bought and what would not. Staff had been treated in a more patronising, and less responsible way than were many children with pocket money. The loosening of the purse-strings was such a breakthrough that it brought applause at the principal teachers' meeting when the change was announced.

Despite these clear advances, the tensions were still simmering. They began to come to a head when I noticed, during my frequent strolls round the school, that educational practices were taking place which took me back to my early days at Niddrie Marischal. Part of the curriculum in one department was washing the teacher's car. I had to bring the teacher to heel over this. Children being given a football and sent out to play just to get them out of the room was another unacceptable practice. Sometimes a tacit agreement existed that if the children sat quietly they would be given less academic work to do, and this too had to be stopped. My journeys also uncovered another characteristic of some departments – hoarding new equipment unused. Advisers had given overhead projectors to two departments. These were my favourite educational toy at that time, but they had lain unpacked, either because of lack of skill or of interest. Unfortunately, nobody else had access to 'their' equipment. This attitude led to the creation of the audio-visual department, in which the centralised hardware belonged to all of the staff.

As early as August, there had been a serious flashpoint when I was preparing the appeals for the previous session's set of examination results. To my horror, one of the principal teachers, who did not believe in appeals, had destroyed the evidence. About two or three months later he came into my office, straight from one of the house assemblies, and said that he was appalled at the behaviour of the young people and that if I was not going to change this he wished to resign. I asked him to take a seat and gave him a sheet of headed notepaper and a pen, whereupon he resigned. That was the first and last time, I am happy to report, that anyone tried to pressurise me in this manner.

There was no getting away from it. The cause of the tension was my position on corporal punishment. This position was the driving force behind the policies I was attempting to implement in an effort to make the school less authoritarian.

To this end, I abolished the school rules soon after my arrival. By doing so, I was hoping to remove some of the potential causes of friction. Crisis moments go on all the time at school. 'So and so has broken . . .' The rules do not stop the incidents. They merely create more crises.

Schools do not normally belong to students. The young people often have to cut their way through regulations designed to make the lives of the staff easier and to keep the children in a powerless role. Giving a school over to students sounds easy. I knew it would prove difficult to achieve. I wanted to inculcate into the students respect for each other. I wanted them to understand and follow the maxim: 'I respect you, you respect me, and so let's not behave in a negative way. Don't do to me what you wouldn't like done to you.' Such a code of respect would allow students the freedom to develop in a responsible manner. It would not produce licence. Freedom not licence was basic. A.S. Neill.

It was, of course, not possible to overturn years of authoritarian schooling overnight. There were outbreaks of trouble. The staff were also unsure. They were puzzled about whether or not it would work. As I had removed the friction points, some staff thought that I would be the one to implement any punishments they deemed necessary. I explained that using my authority to resolve trivia would undermine the whole structure when I was required to deal with a serious matter. At no time in history has hanging for minor crimes solved the real malaise in society. Staff for some time tried to corner me, so that I would have to resort to 'the tawse'. In most cases I was able, as Neill would have been, to talk the student into accepting his or her punishment from the class teacher. In a growing number of cases an apology was the solution. Because I was developing an easy relationship with the students, they disliked being sent to me for punishment. They disliked me not smiling. For them, conflict with me was not a challenge and a power struggle.

One clear memory stands out above all the rest. It is of a student known as 'Crazy', who had created havoc in the technical department. Two technical teachers marched him into my office, without prior warning, stating he had stolen a file and demanding that the boy be belted. The student and I looked at each other for a few moments. Then I said, 'Take the file out of your pocket, and give it back.' A brief eye-to-eye contact, a pause which went on forever, then it happened – the student followed my instructions and handed back the file. It was pure Neill and it worked!

When students were brought to me over matters of discipline, I tried to treat them fairly and to persuade them to accept the form of punishment. My refusal to use corporal punishment meant that punitive measures ranged from lines or detention to the final deterrent, being sent home and having access to classes refused until one or both parents came into school to discuss the problem, a practice which was not common in 1973. This allowed me, or the guidance staff, to have direct contact with the parents of difficult children.

By 1972 Craigroyston had stopped sending senior students to the local sixth-year school and had slowly, in an unofficial way, built up a small top, with a few students who were preparing to go to further education. These students had previously been prefects and were part of the discipline structure. I abolished this system and let these teenagers be, quite simply, students, not quasi-quislings on 'the teachers' side'. Again, this caused ripples among some of the staff but, in fact, proved successful.

My initial relationship with the students was difficult to assess, but one incident which made a lasting impression on me was strolling into a classroom to find the students leaping to their feet and repeating in a chorus, 'Good morning, Sir!' It was the first and last time that this happened. At the next staff meeting, I explained that this form of address was in direct contradiction to the atmosphere I was trying to create. I impressed upon the staff that, as I wished to be on first-name terms with staff, it seemed rather pointless to have this formal relationship with the students. Being around at the class changeover and at the beginning of the school day made me a recognisable figure in Craigie. I hoped that the casual dress and the friendly approach made contact between myself and the students different. Most of them were friendly and smiling as they came into school. Very quickly I became known as 'the Heidie' and behind my back as 'Big John Wayne', a name passed down for 20 years and still used when I meet former Craigie students today.

The students were well aware of their position in society and of the adverse publicity that appeared about Pilton in the media. The more I saw of this, the more I was convinced that most of the aggression between staff and students was the result of this belittling, conscious or unconscious.

In allowing them access to their school, most of the students reacted in a positive way. There was a minority who were unable to accept the freedom and were only able to interpret it as a licence to do as they wished.

Some students saw the removal of the dress code as an excuse to annoy teachers, and this caused friction which required disciplinary action. Gradually, the ethos of the school changed from a fearful to a friendly environment. It did not happen overnight, but it was achieved more quickly than I had thought possible.

If an existing order is taken away, it is essential that another replaces it. Without order, there is chaos. I had taken away the rules, the prefectorial system, the authoritarian nature of the school, and the role of the head as the ultimate belter. I replaced it with a code of respect, but there needed to be a structure inside which this would work. If the status quo had rested on punishment, the system I was trying to implement rested on counselling, talking out, and encouragement. The vital link in the changes I was introducing was the guidance system.

CHAPTER NINE

Talking the Blues Away

Craigie had an established guidance system as it was one of the first Scottish schools to benefit from the implementation of the Scottish Education Department publication *Guidance in Scottish Secondary Schools*, the handiwork of Forsyth McGarrity. This document was an innovative and forward-looking piece of educational thinking. Its implementation was spoiled by the usual British government attitude to educational change. Work it out, implement it, appoint staff. Then, after the process is started, *maybe* think about training.

As a result, there were many hair-raising appointments made throughout Scotland, and many staff were appointed for the wrong reasons. The net result of this was that many staff took a jaundiced view of these non-chalkface workers, who developed friendly relationships with young people. Moreover, the whole concept of guidance was little understood.

The guidance staff were appointed to counsel the students in their academic studies, personal problems and career paths. The guidance system already in place at Craigie when I took up my post had been used as a control mechanism and was heavily reliant on corporal punishment. When I set about changing this, it created tension between myself and the guidance staff. They firmly believed that unless they continued with this system, the whole school would disintegrate. This view, of course, reinforced those of other members of staff, unhappy about the changes. I was always amazed at the arrogance with which the pro-belters saw themselves as holding the whole school together.

Good counselling was the control mechanism I preferred. After all, Neill was a counsellor, probably *the* counsellor. My American experience was my first direct contact with a counselling/guidance system in which specially trained former classroom teachers used their acquired skills to talk out problems with students. In spite of all the bad publicity about American schools, these counsellors worked in a non-confrontational way. This removed the problem from the classroom and de-escalated the confrontations, but it was a solution which was expensive of time. The Maryland counsellors did not teach but were involved in individual or group therapy. This produced friction with the teaching staff over the former's perceived lack of understanding of current life in the classroom.

At Craigmount I had helped Bill Trotter establish a guidance system that gave the staff time but required them to teach social education as well as having a limited teaching timetable in their own discipline. This model was the one to be transplanted into Craigie, but without dedicated and understanding staff the transplant could not have taken root.

My luck held. Craigie was allowed another assistant head, who was to be in charge of the guidance system. Billie Smith was promoted. She was a member of the original Craigroyston guidance staff (or house directors as they were to become known in Craigie). Here was a woman with a pro-child perspective who instinctively empathised with Neillian philosophy. Ann Hyslop, Isobel Leckie and Roy Crichton were appointed as house directors, and Bob Aitchison, already in post as a house director and who had pre-dated me at Craigie, became convinced that what I was trying to do was a more effective route to educating children than was the policy of the previous regime. A team was now in place.

The guidance staff was given a high profile and the time vital to doing their job successfully. We met weekly to thrash out policy. Moves towards co-operation with other agencies involved with children, the Social Work Department, Educational Psychology, the police and the Children's Panel were started at a time when an interdisciplinary approach was not the norm. They had an excellent grasp of the huge social problems with which the students were hampered. Tolerance became the keynote. The emphasis on attendance and time-keeping changed. Punishment was replaced by understanding. I stood at the front door in the morning to welcome the students as they arrived. I hit upon this idea simply by inverting the traditional role of the teacher at the front gate, belt in hand, awaiting late-comers. In my early years of teaching, this had been a common sight and one which I found traumatic and demeaning for both staff and students. During one of my student teaching placements, I had seen the children belted in the playground for arriving after the bell. I turned this practice on its head, welcoming the children, late-comers and all.

The introduction of the guidance system resulted in the addition of social education to the curriculum. Social education offered the guidance staff the opportunity to tackle teenage social problems, adolescent tensions, and give academic and career advice.

To begin with, the guidance staff had difficulty grasping that talking was the essence of social education. Scottish education was so steeped in written work that they kept asking for exercise books. I said, 'No, no, no, that's not social education. I don't want them writing in your subject area, I want them to talk.' I refused to provide the staff with jotters for the students, and this led to a degree of friction. Gradually, things became easier as the guidance staff, having picked up what I was trying to do, steadily, one by one, phased out corporal punishment. Looking back, I know I was very fortunate that the guidance staff accepted my philosophy. Had they not done so, the whole system would have collapsed.

The guidance staff had a vital job to do in the school, and as a result acquired a high profile. This caused reaction from the subject principal teachers, who felt that the balance had moved. It had. I was moving towards guidance and discrete subjects having equal status. It was a logical move in Neillian terms to promote the position of the staff who were at the heart of the child-centred aspect of Craigie. The enhancement of the house directors' position also gave a clear signal to the remainder of the staff that counselling work was as vital as academic work.

However, I would not repeat the American mistake of not having the counsellors teach. The guidance staff had to teach, not only in order to prevent the American-style accusations but also to raise the status of guidance to the level of the traditional subjects. Their role in school was to be different from that of traditional teachers. They needed time for one-to-one counselling of students, and I made that time available by increasing their non-contact class time. This was not a popular move.

I used the strategy of new appointments whenever a vacancy arose to appoint staff who were more in line with my own thinking. Whether they had read Neill or not, I do not know. It was not a question I asked at the interview. But word of what I was trying to do was filtering across the city, and applications for posts came more often from like-minded people.

I was able to move to the next phase of development – a gradual progression to the elimination of corporal punishment. Guidance staff used their time to talk to students and help them with their problems. This proved successful. Had it not been, the move to a non-corporal punishment situation would never have been possible. The staff found the early transition difficult. Close relationships that were developing between the staff and myself prevented the whole experiment from foundering.

The house directors had direct contact with their own group tutors, the Craigie name for the teachers who registered the attendance of the children each day. This allowed the changes in the approach to the students to spread and was probably one of the reasons for the rapid change in the Craigie ethos.

When the Scottish Education Department decided it was time for change, it established three working parties, the Munn, Dunning and Pack committees which all reported in 1977. The first two, which dealt with the exam system and curriculum, have had a major impact, but the Pack Report dealing with children and their treatment in school lies on a shelf in St Andrew's House collecting dust. This is an interesting and depressing statement about Scottish education.

When visiting Craigie, the Pack Committee made positive comments on the atmosphere and the friendly relationship between staff and students. They were surprised at the attendance rates, which were above that of most of the schools they had visited. As they departed, the headteacher on the committee took me aside to relate an incident. During an interview with a group of fourth-year leavers, one student surprised them when he stated that teachers in Craigie really cared for the students in their tutor groups. This student had taken a day off, and when he returned there were no recriminations, only genuine concern about his possible health and family problems. This caring attitude was the hallmark of Craigie group tutors.

CHAPTER TEN

The Curriculum is the Message

Just as a caring rather than a punitive guidance system was necessary to my vision, so also was a rethinking of the curriculum. Within the state system attending classes could not be optional. But there was nothing to stop me from altering the curriculum to suit the needs of the students. In the early 1970s, the Scottish Certificate of Education Examination Board provided national exams at S4, S5 and S6. These exams provided the passport to jobs and further education. They were designed to be attainable by only a minority, thereby keeping in place the hierarchic system of achievement. For thousands of students all over the country these exams were as remote as the moon, and yet the entire system was driven by them. Consequently, for many students school was a drudgery of watered-down academic work which bored them, and at which they failed.

Much of the tension and antagonism that was a running sore in the education system was the result of young people struggling with academic activities, in which they could see no point. I set out to change this. The exam classes would, of course, continue. As long as the system outside school valued exams, I had a duty to encourage those capable of passing them. In my view, however, I also had a duty to provide a suitable educational experience for the students for whom academic success was not possible.

To alter the curriculum is a daunting task because it creates conflict not only with the staff but also with the bureaucrats in the local authority and the inspectors of Her Majesty's schools. I felt that the time to challenge the system was right, since some more clear-sighted members of the educational establishment had come to realise that changes were inevitable. I had no clear idea of what could replace the existing curriculum, but I wanted to expand the students' experiences and give them choices that they could then reject or accept.

The curriculum is the major control mechanism in any education system. It, in turn, is controlled by the exam system, external or internal, and implemented via the timetable. A secondary-school timetable is very complex, but its very complexity has often been used, quite deliberately, as the excuse to prevent change.

Neill solved this problem by allowing children the space and time to play out their childhood. He felt this prepared them to cope with the normal external exam system, when they were ready. This solution was not possible in the state system, where children could not attend classes if and when it suited them. The curriculum had to be altered, and in such a way as to allow the students freedom of choice, enrichment of experience and, wherever possible, a qualification which would enhance employment opportunities. In the 1970s unemployment was not yet the norm for the young people of the Scottish council estates. Many 'Free Schools' sprang up at this time and, mistaking freedom for licence, failed to understand that they were depriving the students of employment opportunities by underplaying the importance of academic study. This mistake would not be repeated at Craigie, where the students already had enough of life's handicaps without the additional one of being sold short at school.

My geographical training had given me a deep interest in field work and taking students out of school. The Illich conception of de-schooling – that a classroom need not be four walls – was the essence of the theory that students should explore the environment. Edinburgh, with its parks, rivers, foreshore, museums and galleries, offered a perfect study area. There was also my acknowledgment of Neill's philosophy that students should not be tied to desks. Added to this amalgam of ideas was my own belief that students have to be trained to observe – hence the appearance of the ubiquitous worksheet. This was to become the tool to help students observe and give staff a focus for visits. Over the years it became a running joke that Hugh would not let anyone out of the building without clipboards and worksheets.

One of my own first worksheets was related to the geology, flora and fauna of Queen's Park. This royal park is a green lung in the centre of the city. The choice was partially stimulated by the sight of a trail of Edinburgh burghers leading their families up the well-worn track to the summit of Arthur's Seat on a Sunday afternoon. This experience was, for a variety of reasons, denied to many Craigie students. In a sense the staff became surrogate parents leading the children up Arthur's Seat as part of their education. This fitted perfectly with the atmosphere developing at Craigie.

The de-schooling programme had its difficult moments. I remember Ken MacAskill (principal teacher of English) and a group of students returning from a walk in the Pentlands, exclaiming, 'The hills are on fire!' This was somewhat of an exaggeration. The students had set alight a clump of whins. Fortunately, quick action by Ken saved the Pentlands! Another group visiting an art exhibition knocked over and broke a piece of pottery. Chaos! The irate artist arrived in my office. What could I do but pay for the broken pottery?

Colin Mitchell, the only member of the Craigie staff who has, to date, been promoted to headteacher, was a keen de-schooler. One afternoon, while working with his animal-studies class at the Union Canal at Ratho, he was shocked when a white-faced student reported that he had found a dead body. Quickly, the police were summoned. Everyone was interviewed. As the subdued class boarded the minibus, the investigating officer took aside the student who had found the body and told him with a straight face, 'If no one claims the body in a fortnight it will be yours, son.' Maybe the policeman realised that this was a biology trip for collecting specimens.

Edinburgh Zoo was an excellent classroom for the animal-studies class. The students were always welcome, especially after their success with the elephant. This elephant had refused to come out of its house for some time, and the staff were worried about its health. A Craigie student came to the rescue. He went into the elephant house and gave the animal a ticking off, whereupon it

71

gave a trumpet and walked outside. Alas, George did not become a vet!

An incident in the Botanic Gardens exemplifies one of the problems we had to confront. Some park keepers shouted at the students, and the result was an outburst of Pilton's four-letter words. If Scottish working-class children are spoken to in an aggressive manner they will reply in the same mode. This was a learning experience for all of us on the Craigie staff. Incidents like these might have resulted in a return to the classroom had not so many of us believed in the value of de-schooling.

The next addition to the curriculum was the Edinburgh Festival and Fringe programme of visits. In the past city schools had used both cultural events mainly for senior students who were interested in music and/or drama. In 1973 Joyce and I attended a Fringe production by an American dance company, the Pilobocus Dance Theatre, in the hall of St Thomas of Acquin's School. We were impressed by the athleticism and gymnastic ability of the dancers. After the performance, I sought out the director and asked if he would put on a show for the Craigie students. To my delight he agreed. We struck a price, and the next week we transported 150 students to the production. This was the start of the Craigie Festival and Fringe programme, which to this day has allowed every student to see at least one show each year, either in Craigie or at a theatre venue. This was another example of opening doors for students and exposing them to other life experiences. The 1974 programme gives an indication of the breadth of the annual Festival and Fringe undertaking. The programme involved a massive load on staff time and logistics and was paid for out of

Craigroyston High School Festival and Fringe Programme, 1974

Title of production	In/out of school	Year group	No. of Students
Judas	out	5/6	40
Sorry and All That	out	5/6	12
Lorry	out	5/6	6
Collage	in	3/4	150
Right On	out	4	80
Liz	out	3	118
American Mime	in	4	40
Macbeth	out	5/6	60
Hero	in	2	320
Heartbreaker	out	3/4	150
Treasure Island	out	1/2	350
Stagefright	out	3	9
Big Al	out	3/4/5/6	10
Mama	out	5/6	12
Black America	out	5/6	12
Stage Play	out	5/6	12
Rock and Roll High School	out	5/6	5
One Flew Over the Cuckoo's Nest	out	5/6	25
Flying Blind	out	5/6	25
Der Vampyr	out	5/6	6
James Galway Concert	out	3/4/5/6	20
Exhibitions – Various	out	3/4	300

the School Trust Fund. It also set the tone for cultural visits to and from Craigie over the rest of the session, encouraging departments to extend the scope of their activities. The students adapted well to being taken to these alien environments, illustrating how they responded to being placed in a position of trust in public places.

Pilton families, in the main, do not participate in the annual Edinburgh arts jamboree. Never have I been more acutely aware of this alienation than when one girl returning from a theatre visit, her eyes shining with excitement, asked, 'Am I allowed to take my Mum to see the play tonight?'

CHAPTER ELEVEN

The CSE Road Show

Anyone trying to shift the direction of an organisation or a system needs two things: to be in the right place at the right time and luck!

The curriculum model had been improved, but it still had a major weakness. There were no suitable academic courses for the bulk of Craigie's students. This problem would become greater in 1973 with the raising of the school leaving age, the spectre haunting many Scottish teachers, who foresaw their problems mounting as a cohort of reluctant 15-year-olds were forced to stay in school for another year. The main teaching union, the Educational Institute of Scotland (EIS) was trying to stall the change until an appropriate exam system was in place, while the government, as always, wanted to make the change and then find a way to make it work. Some educators, on the other hand, were trying to find a solution. One such person was Eric Ferguson, who invited me to join a group of Edinburgh heads who were visiting Barnsley, in the West Riding of Yorkshire. There we observed the pioneering work of Sir Alex Clegg in the CSE examination system, and in particular the Mode 3 aspect.

The focus of the visit was a school in the mining village of Grimethorpe, where we talked to both staff and students. The staff explained that, for them, the Mode 3 courses had three strengths: they were written by the school staff to suit the ability of the students, they were graded internally by the staff, and the results were checked by external moderators. The courses, although written in the school, were validated by the local regional exam board. They were based on a network of aims and objectives, which immediately reminded me of Bill Williams's work at North Bethesda and Tilden Junior High Schools. The courses were a compliment to the professionalism of the staff who had created them decades before ownership was a buzz word in educational jargon. Here was a solution to Craigie's curriculum problem; if it worked in Grimethorpe it would surely work in Pilton. The Yorkshire visit also included my first visit to a community high school, my response to which was tucked away for the future.

Returning to Craigie, there was a full-scale job to be done. The principal teachers had to be persuaded that they could write the CSE Mode 3 courses for their own students. Before everyone wasted time and energy, permission was required from both the local and national authorities to allow us to proceed. They proved reluctant to allow a Scottish school to attach itself to an English examination system. This irritated me because this was not, of course, the case for those bastions of English culture, the Scottish public schools, when they entered students for the English A levels.

After much telephoning and correspondence, agreement was reached with Eric Ferguson and HMI Dr W. A. Gatherer to allow Craigie to experiment with the CSE system. It would be controlled by the Northern Regional Examination Board in Newcastle and begin with the 1973 diet of courses. This agreement, assisted by Eric and Bill, who were to become major supporters of Craigie, indicated that some of those in authority were searching for a solution to the problem caused by the raising of the school leaving age.

The next task was to train the principal teachers in writing aims and objectives for the construction of courses based on Bill Williams's pamphlet on how to write educational objectives. I phoned a friend at North Bethesda Junior High, who dispatched a dozen copies of Bill's pamphlet. This was a significant breakthrough in in-service training. Principal teachers came together not to receive information but to be trained for a specific educational purpose. I had now placed myself in the role of an adult educator.

As time wore on, folklore grew round my new role. Wild stories circulated of no one being allowed to leave the in-service training meeting until he or she could write aims and objectives! My version of the story is different, but there was a nucleus of truth in the legend.

A series of integrated thematic courses were developed across school departments. Into the courses went material to suit the needs of the students in creative arts, outdoor education, environmental studies or technology. The system we created allowed the students, with guidance from their house directors, to select subjects which would give them the whole of their curriculum and in

CSE Mode 3 Courses

Course Title	Date started	Period allocation	Subjects involved
1 Communications	1973	15	English, mathematics, science, art, theatre arts
2 Child-care	1973	15	Home economics, human biology, child development, child-care, art
3 Outdoor studies	1973	15	Science, outdoor pursuits, social studies, art
4 Technology	1973	15	Technical, science, art, social studies
5 Distribution and the consumer	1973	15	Commerce, social studies, art and design
6 Creative arts	1973	15	Art, home economics, technical, music, theatre arts, human movement
7 Community service	1973	15	Home economics, human biology, social studies
8 Environmental studies	1973	15	Science, social studies, art
9 Office Practice	1975	15	Commercial practice and office organisation, typing, social studies, drama
10 European studies	1975	15	French, home economics, social studies, human movement
11 Animal studies	1975	15	Science, technical, art, geography
12 Catering	1979	15	Home economics, science, social studies, art, languages, business studies

addition CSE Mode 3 English and maths. It was to be a success.

Families became known for the thematic courses chosen by their offspring. Suddenly there emerged 'outdoor education' families or 'animal studies' families. To try to ensure success, class size was limited to 20, proving what teachers can achieve when they are working with classes of a reasonable size. This number also facilitated the use of the school minibuses for the de-schooling aspect of each course.

The catering course, devised by Mel Campbell, principal teacher of home economics, became so successful that a commercial catering service was established. The Craigie Caterers successfully ventured into the marketplace as outside caterers for a number of public functions. The most prestigious was the weekend conference of the International Federation of Women Lawyers.

All the courses were checked and verified by the Northern Regional Exam Board, which also helped in the teething stages with further in-service training on aims and objectives. It was a professional system but, unfortunately, it did not suit the government. Gradually, it was run down, mainly because there was too much teacher input in the marking and assessment and not enough central control. This was a political decision, which in my view was wrong and which adversely affected the school and education in Scotland in general. Nevertheless, in its heyday CSE Mode 3 was successful and gave terrific impetus to the developments in Craigie. It became the keystone for all of the school's innovations and became known collectively to the staff as the Craigie Curriculum (see Appendix D). A valid measure of CSE was the sense of purpose it gave the students, the feeling that they mattered as much as the students following Ordinary Grade and Higher Grade courses.

Several students who completed their CSE courses stayed on for a fifth and sixth year, thereby underlining Neill's point that people can achieve academically, if and when they are motivated.

When I meet ex-students they normally open the conversation with their field trips. Invariably, they then go on to tell me with joy that they have a certificate which they have kept from school. It's a CSE certificate. One such student came to the 30–year anniversary party for ex-students. He came over to me and said, 'Thanks for giving me the chance, Hughie. Nobody else ever did. I've got a certificate in the house to prove I could do it.' The courses succeeded. The students were hungry for success, and they got it simply because the staff were committed and wrote programmes to suit the Craigie students. CSE was teacher written and, in that, it opened up new ground in Scotland.

Of course, not all the courses were perfect and there were times when it did not work, but the initial results were excellent and students achieved way beyond our greatest expectations, so much so that people further afield in Scottish education became interested in what we were doing. I suddenly found myself, less than three years in the job, on a lecturing circuit organised by the Scottish Curriculum Centre for Studies in School Administration, explaining to headteachers how to implement CSE courses. This meant that many teachers from various parts of the country heard my views on CSE courses, and, as a result, the school became a *de facto* curriculum-development centre with numerous

80

visitors wishing to find out about CSE, see classes in operation and take material away.

During the development of CSE Forsyth McGarrity came to Craigroyston unannounced. He needed evidence of interesting work in maths for Willie Ross, the Secretary of State. I said, 'You have come to the right place. Jim MacDonald is a wonderful maths teacher. He is doing all sorts of innovative work with the students.' And he was. I used to play a trick with the first year. I would say, 'Put up your hands and tell me what subjects you like.' I was amazed by the number of them who liked maths. This was quite against the norm, but nevertheless true because of the way Jim taught maths. I introduced Forsyth McGarrity to Jim and a package of Craigroyston maths worksheets went off to London to show the Secretary of State what maths teaching could be about. Whenever I saw Willie Ross on television after that, I could picture him sitting at a desk in Dover House, doing Craigie's maths worksheets!

Most Lothian Region schools became involved in CSE Mode 3, as well as schools as far apart as Dumfries, Fife, Grampian and the Borders. There must have been more than 100 schools connected with the Northern Regional Exam Board, and I am convinced that this number would have been greater had Strathclyde not taken the decision to remain outwith the CSE structure.

Here was a Labour administration making a statement via their officials to legislate against the children of those who had voted them into power. Had Strathclyde gone with CSE, in my view, the entire face of education in Scotland would now be different. CSE, not Standard Grade, would have been the way forward from Ordinary Grade. It is interesting, of course, to note that the Standard Grade slogan, 'a certificate for all', was born directly out of CSE. Perhaps that is the measure of its success – in official-speak. Mode 3 was the innovation that worked and made the jobs of the teachers easier. Moreover, by asking teachers to write the courses, their professional status and ability was acknowledged.

Once CSE was seen inside the school as successful and identified outside the school as successful, and the staff felt that it was theirs (in modern jargon they owned the courses), it was much easier for me to make suggestions for adding other new ideas to the Craigie Curriculum. When, for instance, I crystallised my thinking about community schooling there was very little resistance; staff were prepared to acknowledge that I could take the right initiatives and that my ideas were not as crazy as they at first sounded. In running any organisation, there has to be credibility. When I look at some of the pioneers in education, it seems to me that they distanced themselves from, and so lost, the staff by asking for quantum leaps before they had made the small steps. I tried very hard not to do that, but I know I was lucky in having the Craigie staff.

CSE was child centred. Scottish teachers were crying out for something to cope with the raising of the school leaving age. The timing was my stroke of luck. I cared about those reluctant 15-year-olds staying on for another year of what they saw as pointless academic courses. CSE gave me the chance to shift the curriculum and to construct a new one for the less academic children. This is what I saw in Barnsley. To so many heads, these children did not matter. This is nowhere more obvious than when I remember that, of the whole group of headteachers who went to Barnsley, I was the only one who came back and tried to do something about it.

But a vision remains a vision until it is functioning, and without the staff moving with me CSE would not have been possible. To the staff, for the vast amount of work they put in to provide good courses to enable our students to succeed, the praise due is enormous.

CHAPTER TWELVE

The Walls Come Tumbling Down

Outdoor education really developed because of my geographical background. At Edinburgh University field trips were an essential part of the geography course, reaching a peak for me in my final year when I completed a dissertation on a month's field work in the Orkney Islands. One of the few enjoyable experiences at Moray House had been a field week at the Aviemore Centre. Early in my teaching career, I had been fortunate to meet Betty Knowles, the head of geography at Falkirk High when I was there. She was committed to taking students to youth hostels to study geography in the field. From this geography-specific activity, I saw the potential and began to consider possible avenues for widening the experience beyond geography.

In casual conversation with a friend one day, I learned that Melville College, one of Edinburgh's exclusive schools, had taken the whole of the third year away simultaneously. For a week, education had simply moved

84

to youth hostels and other centres in Scotland. I thought this a superb idea. I tried to introduce it at Liberton and at Craigmount, but each time I only succeeded in taking away the geographers. The heads would not sanction a trip for the whole year group. They could see the rationale for a geographer going into the field, but they could not see any further.

At Liberton I organised many excursions. One of the earliest had worked very well. Billie Smith, one of the staff who went with me, had been very excited by the experience and told the head that it had been fantastic. The children had got so much out of it. Her praise made it possible for me to run other excursions during term time and in the holidays.

In those days Scottish schools had a lady adviser, a member of staff appointed to look after the girls. At Liberton the lady adviser tried to block certain girls from going on these trips with me. They would cause mayhem. I did not agree. I had a rapport with many of these girls, to the extent that quite a number of them were our babysitters. Fortunately, the head sided with me, and although this caused tension between myself and the lady adviser it did mean that I could put into practice my notion that what was worthwhile for the academic elite was worth while for all.

At Craigmount, Bill Trotter went along with the idea so far, but he could not grasp the nettle and allow all the children to go out in term time to work on a non-subject-specific basis. Then I reached Craigroyston, and at last there was nobody to stop me. There was no head-teacher to say, 'No, you can't do it!' I was determined that Craigroyston was going to have a field trip and it would be for the entire third year. I had decided this during the months of preparation prior to taking up the appointment at Craigroyston, but I was unsure as to how I would announce it to the staff.

Once again fate had taken a hand. On that first day, at the meeting for members of staff wishing to take part in the outdoor-education weekend at Lagganlia, I had said how pleased I was that so many staff were willing to take part in outdoor pursuits, as it would make it much easier to run the programme I had in mind for the following May. Right from Day One, I was committed to the S3 field trip!

Again, these field weeks had to be task oriented. As both Joyce and I were geographers, we used many weekends on outings with our own children to visit centres and then prepare worksheets. The staff accepted the idea of a week-long trip. Many of the younger staff liked it. So did many of the staff who, themselves, enjoyed outdoor pursuits. The important thing was that there were enough staff supportive of the idea to make it work.

I think what finally won round even the most entrenched was the fact that for many of the Pilton children these field weeks were their only holiday. Just as outdoor education in the timetable allowed the surrogate parents to lead the children across hillsides, to canoe up rivers and to walk on beaches, so the field trips provided an experience new for so many. Holidays away from home, so common in the middle class, were a distant fantasy for most of our students. Of course, field trips are not only of value for children in deprived areas. Their aim is an enrichment of life.

Occasionally, the children did not enjoy a trip but that did not invalidate the idea. The point was that they experienced living away from home, with their peers and their teachers, and learned to accept or reject from a position of knowledge. Just as the Edinburgh Festival and Fringe is theirs to accept or reject, so also is the Scottish countryside. On this point precisely turns my rejection of any suggestion that what we were doing was patronising. I was not saying 'My middle-class way is better.' I was saying, 'Here is another way of life. You can choose it, you can take pieces of it. You can reject it. But here it is. Try it.'

In the early stages of trying to develop outdoor education at Craigroyston, I attended a Regional in-service at Benmore Outdoor Education Centre near Dunoon. One of the lecturers was Robert Davies, headteacher of the George Pinder School in Scarborough. This school was committed to outdoor education, both as a discipline and as a stimulus for many of the school subjects. I was intrigued.

I got in touch with Robert Davies, and he was delighted to invite a group of Craigie staff to see the school programme working. The school was more steeped in outdoor education than we ever imagined. Not only did it own its own outdoor centre, but it also produced much of its own equipment in school departments. Here was education tied to both industry and to the environment in a creative and worthwhile way.

Underpinning all this, the school had adopted the three Cs, confident, capable and co-operative, as its motto. With a name like Craigie, it was a golden opportunity to develop the idea. On our return home, the three Cs plus the addition of a fourth, caring, became the motto for Craigie.

The success of the field weeks can be measured in many ways. The first was that the staff co-operated enthusiastically in the programme. Without their enthusiasm, trips would not have continued for 20 years. Staff knew that their relationships with students improved. The students gained a great deal from the field trips, so much so that there was a gradual expansion of the programme, to include the first and second years.

Craigroyston High School Field-Trip Programme 1982–83

Year	Venue	Days	Students	Staff
1	Abington	3	51	4
	Aberfoyle	3	78	6
	West Linton	3	51	4
2	Abernethy	5	64	5
	Dalguise	5	56	5
	Benmore	5	23	3
	Lagganlia	5	32	3
3	Abernethy	5	34	4
	Arran	5	22	4
	Dykehead	5	12	4
	Stanley Nairne	5	18	4
	Ardgarten	5	16	3
	Rowardennan	5	15	3
	Bernice	5	11	2
	Whernside	5	10	3
	Aboyne	5	18	4
	Lagganlia	5	29	4

In the early years of the expansion, students used a community resource, 'the Ratho Retreat'. This was

introduced to the school by former city counsellor Vic
Lindsay and was owned and run by the Pilton Central
Association, an umbrella community organisation, as a
holiday centre to allow people living in the area an opportunity to experience a different environment. This community project was parallel to the school's aim, and for
a number of years Ratho was where the youngest
students had their first residential experience outwith
north-west Edinburgh. In the early days some of the
staff regarded the trips as a disruption of the normal
educational process. They labelled them a waste of time
detracting from the real work. My reply was always that
a flu epidemic could keep the children away from school
for longer and had no educational advantages. Field trips
did! They were an essential component of the Craigie
Curriculum.

The success of the early field trips, and the de-
schooling programme which resulted from it, led to the
rapid growth in outdoor education. In 1973 Lothian
Region agreed to appoint John Wells, a member of the
geography department, as assistant principal teacher of
outdoor education (ODE). This was in recognition of his
work in helping to develop ODE at Craigie and was the
first instance of a promoted teacher without an actual
department.

The field trips threw up a variety of legends. Some
were funny and many underlined the problems the
students faced in their own environment. One recurring
incident was when a youngster unable to settle at an
outdoor centre, and with no real concept of distance and
time, would set off to walk home to Pilton. Normally he
or she would be shadowed by a member of staff and

within the hour the 'escapee' was back, ready to participate for the rest of the week.

Scottish eating habits were challenged. In a centre
in South Wales, a student was heard to comment on the
menu, as she nibbled her lettuce, 'I didn't know I was
coming to a blankety blank health farm.'

On another occasion in the Cairngorms, I met Bob
Aitchison and a party coming from the opposite direction.
Unknown to me, Bob had told the students that if they
didn't behave he'd send for the 'Heidie', who would
arrive and sort them out. As his merry band strolled
along, I appeared over the horizon as if summoned. This
'miracle' had quite an effect on their behaviour for the
remainder of the trip.

For many staff, including myself, the trips have,
over the years, provided a treasure of happy memories.
For many students, the field weeks are their most vivid
memory of school, and indeed a number have found such
real pleasure in the outdoors that they have incorporated
it into their lives, to the extent that two former students,
Peter Gardiner and Joey Gowans, upskilled themselves
to outdoor-education-instructor level. Joey then
returned to Craigie as a para-professional attached to the
outdoor education department.

All of this created a hefty financial headache. At the
beginning we charged the students ten pence for the use
of the minibuses, but this created more problems than it
solved. It was difficult to collect the money. In line with
trying to be an enabler, I thought there had to be an
easier way. Out of that was born the notion of a trust
fund. At a principal teachers' meeting I laid out my
strategy. People just sat there shaking their heads. One

man said, 'It will never work. You will never do it.' I said, 'Of course we will.'

This, like all trust funds, was a sum of money invested on behalf of the trustees. In Craigie's case the interest would be used to underwrite outdoor education and travel. The trust fund was set up in 1974, and, over the years, was increased to a significant figure. In the days of high interest, this meant that the school could safely underwrite the field trips and the minibuses needed to operate the de-schooling policy.

We were determined that no one would be excluded on financial grounds. Our aim was to raise enough money so that every child could have one Festival or Fringe experience annually and outdoor education as part of the school week. I was lucky. It was the 1970s when it was easy to acquire money. The local authority was support-ive. Eric Ferguson was very good to the school. He was delighted to see Craigroyston developing and giving a lead to other more prestigious schools in the city. I also remorselessly tapped friends who were affluent until it reached the stage when they would turn when they saw me coming. One eminent former student, Gordon Stra-chan, was once overheard saying, 'Every time I see that man it costs me money.'

The upshot was that a very healthy trust fund grew quite quickly, and the interest was spent annually. This continues to be the practice.

CHAPTER THIRTEEN

The Alternative Craigie

One of the problems facing the school was what to do with the very difficult, the disturbed and the simply outrageous students. What could the school do? The presence in the school of such students, with whom all housing-estate schools are familiar, strengthened the pro-corporal-punishment lobby. They were able to argue that these students would be impossible to contain after a ban on corporal punishment. As I saw it, there was a small number of young, disadvantaged people in the school who, when faced with a normal educational experience, felt so threatened that they disrupted the work of their calmer colleagues. The solution had to be supportive not punitive. Solutions were sought, and after discussions with Peter Priestley, the head of Psychological Services, it was agreed that my proposal of setting up a unit to be called School House be investigated. To this, youngsters not suited to mainstream education would go. The pressure on the teaching staff in the main building would be removed and the rest of the students would no longer face severe class disruption. A 'sin bin' this was not! All students had a right to education, and it was up to the professionals to provide it in a form accessible to them. If we were unable to do this, the Local Authority policy would continue, i.e. disruptive students would be removed from school and home and sent to a List D school, an institution in the eyes of the world loosely equated with a juvenile jail. I was aware that similar projects had ended up neither adequate nor appropriate. I was determined to get it right.

There were two existing ways forward. One was to place the unit in the main school, but this would have made it difficult to develop a different ethos and, more importantly, an appropriate curriculum. The other model would be a composite one serving other schools, but the drawback here would be that the unit would have no sense of belonging to an identifiable place. We decided on our way forward. The unit would belong solely to Craigie and would be situated off campus. As with the earlier developments in the main school, I was convinced the answer lay in the curriculum and possibly in individualised programmes of work for each student.

Where to locate the new School House raised a problem. Our choice was outwith the school but inside the community. This would allow the staff freedom to develop a suitable ethos. In a sense, this was not a difficult problem because there were many empty houses in the catchment area. The first site offered was a flat in one of the high-rise blocks, suitable for six to ten students. The flat was gradually equipped, and Mary Foreman, a teacher from Special Education, was appointed to be in charge.

All did not go according to plan, however. When

Mary arrived to open the School House on the first day, she was unable to do so. The locks had been plastered over by the local residents. One of the students to be enrolled in the unit lived in the high rise, and the residents felt that one such young person was quite enough. They did not want another six or seven. Here was an impasse. It looked as if the project was still-born. However, the local priest, Father McAllister, who liked the idea of the project, found us a house at 32 Ferry Road Avenue. He took the responsibility for all the liaison work, and we were able to establish School House without any further community objections. This was a salutary lesson in the importance of good communications with the community.

School House worked because it was limited to Craigroyston students. At no time were students from other schools admitted. There were many attempts by the Children's Panel to dispose of awkward cases by sending them to us. Local social workers also tried to use School House to solve other schools' problems. The staff were adamant that School House was not an ad hoc List D school for the rest of Edinburgh. Pilton had more than its own share of problems without adding to them from outwith the area. The students who went to School House were identified by the guidance staff, but the final placement was the result of discussion between Mary Foreman, Billie Smith, myself and the parents. Once an agreement was reached, no student was placed in School House without the parents being invited to visit and talk with Mary Foreman.

The curriculum constructed by Mary allowed students to work at their own speed, i.e. individualised learning, and success was often rewarded with time at play. Needless to say, there was no corporal punishment. This was a very Neillian approach to the process of learning, which reduced the pressure on many of our more disturbed students.

It was vital to the success of School House that it was located 'along the road'. Its style of education would have been much more difficult to achieve in the main building, where Mary could not have operated with her small number of students in the unique style necessary.

The curriculum was enriched by materials from the departments and, in the early days, by visits by teaching staff. The latter was only established after a stormy staff debate about whether or not I had the authority to ask staff to work in School House. The debate concluded with the view that School House was indeed an integral part of the school. Later on, students came to the main building with Mary for work in practical subjects.

Once students were settled in School House, they were able to negotiate a return to those mainstream classes taught by staff with whom they had a positive relationship. This tactic also placed the youngsters in the position of trusties, in that they had to walk the quarter-of-a-mile to Craigie unaccompanied. I am not aware that anybody abused the privilege and ran away.

The curriculum that evolved at School House was a microcosm of the Craigie Curriculum. De-schooling in the form of educational visits was the norm, as was out-door education, and eventually a residential experience. The quality and development of the School House staff enabled all this to happen. Without their commitment and exceptional skills, it could not have worked.

School House was a success. It encouraged students to attend school, and many were reintegrated into the main building, where some achieved academic success. One such student in his fifth year and taking Scottish Certificate of Education Highers once remarked, 'Without School House I would have ended up in the slammer.' Many grew into happy individuals holding down jobs, individuals who had benefited by not being removed from their community in their formative years.

In the mid-1970s the area of West Pilton went into an accelerating decline. The poor quality of the post-war housing was becoming an increasing problem. The houses were badly affected by rising damp, and this led to a drift away from the Pilton area. The tenement in which School House was located was no exception, and within a short period all the other flats were vacated. This was not a reflection on the existence of School House but on the quality of the housing. Suddenly the school was faced with an interesting problem. It had to look after six houses instead of the original one. This allowed School House to expand and take in more young people.

A plan was devised for the other flats. The second floor was to be used for a Primary Unit, and one on the upper floor would house a caretaker. The latter would become a residential sanctuary for young people who needed a respite from a crisis situation at home. This latter part of the plan got no further than the paper on which it was written. No agency was interested in inter-agency work at that time.

However, the Primary Unit idea was revived when Craigie developed its relationship with the Bernard van Leer Foundation, and the proposal was incorporated into the original submission to the foundation. The idea behind the Primary Unit was that Scotland is not populated with charming primary children who suddenly

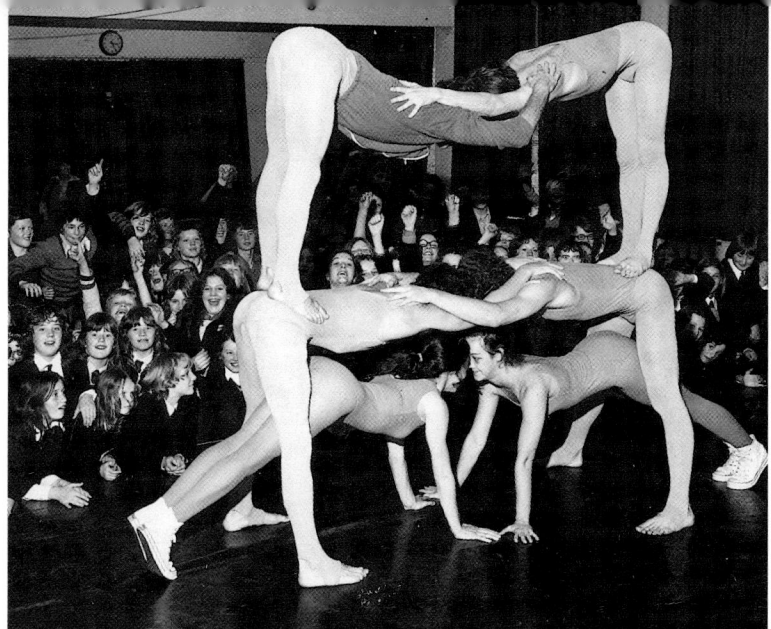

The first Fringe visit, when 250 students were taken to see an American dance company, August 1973 (Scotsman Publications)

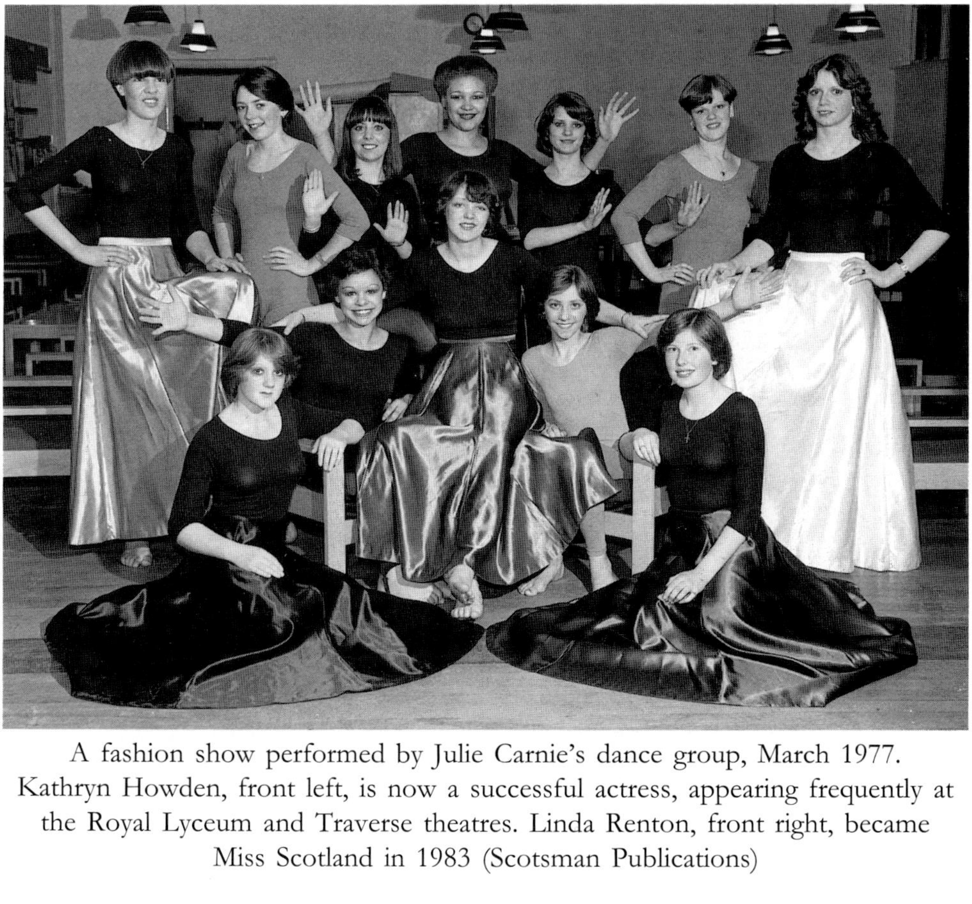

A fashion show performed by Julie Carnie's dance group, March 1977. Kathryn Howden, front left, is now a successful actress, appearing frequently at the Royal Lyceum and Traverse theatres. Linda Renton, front right, became Miss Scotland in 1983 (Scotsman Publications)

The 1976 'Womble'. No wonder residents thought Pilton looked
cleaner. The 25 tons of rubbish were translated into £1,250
(Scotsman Publications)

Local hero Gordon Strachan returns to his old school and is waylaid into signing autographs (Scotsman Publications)

The 1973 staff pantomime, a politically incorrect *Robin Hood* (Scotsman Publications)

Above:
Staff and students celebrate Craigie's Silver Jublilee, 1988
(Maldwyn Stride)

Left:
The launch of the Silver Jubilee balloon race, 1988.
The winning tag was returned from Telemark, Norway
(Pat Coburn)

Craigie field-trippers in the Lost Valley, Glencoe (Des Rubens)

A Craigie 'rock ape' (Des Rubens)

The little people and their mums join the rest of Craigie on the 1984 sponsored walk (Scotsman Publications)

A very young Craigie student with his mum and the 'Heidie'
(Scotsman Publications)

Former students who exhibited their work at the 'After Images'
Exhibition at the City Art Centre in 1985 (Paul Duke)

Staff say 'Goodbye, Mr MacKenzie', June 1993 (Pat Coburn)

evolve into anti-social teenagers in S1. A primary level of School House was necessary for the children who could not cope with mainstream primary education. Time in School House might solve some of the youngsters' problems and, at the same time, prepare them for the transfer to secondary education. The move from primary to secondary is traumatic for most children, and for children with problems it is even more so.

Establishing the unit was surprisingly difficult because at first Craigie's four associate primary schools interpreted the idea as a criticism. After detailed negotiations, ably refereed by Fraser Henderson, it was agreed to experiment with a Primary Unit. There was one major concession, however. The children could not move back and forward to their school, in the way that Craigie students did. Jessie Newton was appointed to the Primary Unit post from the Region's primary sector. The experiment worked. The associate primaries became supportive to such an extent that in no time there was a waiting-list. This resulted in Ian Forrest being appointed to cope with this problem.

Craigie now had an excellent educational outpost, correctly described by a Bernard van Leer visitor as the 'school's liaison post' in the community. Its position outwith the school building allowed the School House staff to develop closer relationships with the parents, who were encouraged to visit and discuss their children. Many of the primary students did successfully transfer to Craigie and complete their secondary education. One day, as I talked to a student at the foot of the spiral staircase, I felt a bang on my shoulders. One of the former Primary Unit students had jumped on to my back, which was his way of expressing a friendly greeting. Even more extraordinary was the fact that the other student continued talking as if nothing unusual had happened. Meanwhile, the first lad went off to his next class. Unusual behaviour for a student and a headteacher, yes. But that child came to school and learned. In a punitive school he would have been expelled.

Another feature of School House was an interdisciplinary approach developed by encouraging social workers, educational psychologists, welfare officers and, when relevant, the police to visit and discuss the needs and behaviour of students.

In time the houses in West Pilton were either to be refurbished by the local authority or sold off to private developers. Ferry Road Avenue was sold to developers who did not want School House in their private housing area. Pressure was applied by the Directorate to move the whole operation into the main school. One company even went so far as to donate to the school new outdoor education equipment. However, the local politicians supported the school, and School House became the only council house in a street of private housing. In order to forestall complaints from the new property-owning neighbours, the council agreed to refurbish School House. When it was complete, there were still complaints but the quality of the refurbished work and the behaviour of the students dispelled the fears of the new residents.

The last extension to School House occurred when it became the base for a home-link teacher. The post was created after a successful application for a grant to the Gulbenkian Foundation in 1989. Dorothy Caddell worked with the nursery classes in the four associate primaries. The strategy was to build up parents' confidence, to convince them of their role as educators, and to ease their child's entry to school. It was moving the Craigie philosophy further down the age range.

The approach of School House to the education of disturbed and difficult students was the forerunner of Lothian Region's Youth Strategy policy. This was a multi-agency approach to the problems presented by disturbed children. Its basic aim was to solve a young person's problems in his or her own community.

The staff of School House lobbied regional officials to adopt their proven model for development in the Region's Youth Strategy plans. They agreed to serve on working parties and study groups, but to no avail. In the end the Region decided to reinvent the wheel and settled for a cumbersome three-tiered, inter-agency committee approach.

CHAPTER FOURTEEN

Lochgelly No More

The mid-1970s saw the beginnings of a ground swell of discussion on the possibility of banning the use of corporal punishment in Scottish schools. Some of the more progressive local authorities, such as Lothian, set up working parties to evaluate the position and to consider alternative forms of disciplinary measures. STOPP (Society of Teachers Opposed to Physical Punishment) set up a Scottish branch based in Glasgow. More important than this was the effect of the November 1980 decision by the European Commission on Human Rights. A case had been brought before the European Courts by two Scottish mothers, who refused to agree to their children being belted. The verdict went against the British government. This was followed by the McGuire case in Strathclyde, which removed from the local authority the right to belt a child. Danny McGuire had been withdrawn from school for 14 months because Strathclyde Regional Council refused to give his parents a guarantee that he would not be belted. In November

1980 his mother won her case. Margaret McGuire was acquitted at Clydebank District Court of the charge of failing to ensure her son attended school. Her son returned to school with the guarantee that his mother had struggled for. This development was particularly exciting for me. In my wildest dreams I had not believed that I might see corporal punishment abolished during my working life.

Against this background things were changing at Craigie. The new atmosphere and the more appropriate curriculum led to a gradual decline in belting. At the request of the local authority, its use had been logged by staff through the period 1973–80. The statistics, which were recorded on a weekly basis, showed a 95 per cent reduction. By the session 1979–80 there were only 95 incidents of corporal punishment at Craigroyston, and only one in the summer term. The time seemed right to debate with staff the possibility of banning the belt completely in Craigie.

During the in-service days at the beginning of the autumn term of 1980, all the staff fora – department, principal-teacher and guidance meetings – were asked to open this debate prior to a full staff meeting. Before the meetings began I indicated that I would accept the democratic decision of the staff. Throughout the day, and at the staff meeting in the library, the arguments raged back and forth. Eventually, a proposal was put forward for an experimental ban of one session and, to my delight, it was carried by a large majority. Craigie had taken one more step along the way towards being a true Neillian school. What to do next was the question – should we tell the students of the decision or simply allow word to percolate? Panic swept through the meeting. Anarchy might ensue from telling the students of our decision. Again, the arguments raged. Eventually, the staff decided that the only honest course was a statement to both students and their parents of our intentions. I was happy with this solution.

Far from there being mayhem, the students reacted well and most parents accepted the decision, although, sadly, over the years a number requested that their child be belted! While an understandable reaction, such an attitude is a sad reflection on Scottish society. During the session, as far as I was aware, there were only two incidents where staff reverted to the belt. Both incidents were resolved after a discussion between myself and the member of staff.

At the start of session 1981–82, the staff reconvened to discuss the experimental session and its success or failure. Before any debate took place, a motion was proposed from the floor by Alex Baillie, the principal teacher of history, to ban corporal punishment. The motion was immediately carried with only two dissenters. Craigie had made this great leap forward several years before the law required it.

On 20 January 1982, Lothian Region's Education Committee took the significant step of banning corporal punishment in all its schools with effect from 2 April 1982.

In the afternoon Bob Cuddihy, an STV reporter, phoned to ask if I was willing to support this decision on the evening's *Scotland Today* programme. I willingly agreed. When I arrived at STV's Edinburgh studios, my confidence was totally undermined. A producer left me in a small, empty studio with the throw-away lines, 'Bob will interview you from Glasgow, Mr Mackintosh. Don't look at the monitor or you will freeze.' For what seemed an eternity, I defended the Region's decision. At the end Bob asked if I thought there would be chaos in Lothian schools.

'No,' I answered confidently. 'No. Young people will accept the challenge of the removal of the belt and thrive in the new non-violent environment.'

The decision to ban the belt in Scotland was a quantum leap, removing the control mechanism on which Scottish education has rested for centuries. I felt the politicians had made the correct decision, but they failed to understand the consequences of their action. There was no replacement or substitute for the tawse. The alternative system of discipline had to be based on discussion, tolerance and a highly trained guidance staff. All of these take teacher time, time away from the classroom, and they take money. These facts were either not understood, or ignored, by politicians, especially those on the right. Time required for the counselling role, essential to the various models of alternative discipline of the 1980s, was not a criterion in the models for staffing Scottish schools. There was a complete lack of understanding that time spent out of class counselling students was not wasted. Such counselling would lead to students being more balanced and therefore more ready to participate in the learning process.

CHAPTER FIFTEEN

Enter the Community – Stage Left

By the mid-1970s the Craigie Curriculum had made a significant difference not only to the ethos but also to the atmosphere of the school. The sense of calm, and of welcome, was regularly commented upon by the many visitors. Two separate HMI inspections were very supportive. One of the inspectors, Alex Nisbet, accorded Craigie the ultimate accolade when he compared its ethos with that which he had found at Kilquhanity House, John Aitkenhead's genuine offshoot of Summerhill. I was very touched when he made this comparison. Had he realised this was the greatest compliment he could have paid to Craigie? It was certainly a high-water mark for me.

I had begun to wonder about the next step. I was anxious lest success led to stagnation. I wanted to prevent Craigie ossifying and losing the momentum that had been built up. Could Craigie influence its community or was that conceit? Was it just an extension of that old-fashioned socialist ideal that compensatory education could alter the outlook of people and lead to the gradual improvement of society?

I turned to the community-school movement. Neill, because of the residential nature of Summerhill, worked within his own school community. Could Craigie open its doors, invite in the local residents and retain its child-centred caring ethos? Could the school, with its spirit of non-violence and of encouragement, become the pulse of the whole community?

Community schooling had been a growing interest since my visit to the West Riding. There had already been a few tentative developments in Pilton. A new community centre had opened adjacent to the school in 1973, with a games hall, as a shared resource. It was used by the school during the day and by the community in the evening. When the centre opened, I argued that it should be part of the school campus, run by a community worker responsible to a community-based committee. This would have produced a campus with a secondary school, a community centre and a playing field, plus the possible inclusion of one of the associate primary schools, which was adjacent to Craigie. This was my original community-school model, and it would have allowed the development of a common ethos across the entire age range.

However, the idea was inexplicably quashed by the director in charge of community education. The director's verdict did not, however, prevent Craigie developing close informal relationships with the community centre. Over the years the chair of the Community Centre Management Committee, Tam Tierney, was a leading force in this development. His ability to cut through red tape was a skill he brought to Craigie again as chair of the School Council. The best examples of our co-operation were the Craigie Club and the Over-Fifties Club. The former was started in Craigie by school staff but eventually moved to the centre. It provided a meaningful evening activity for the students. The development of the Over-Fifties Club reversed the process by settling down in the school and using the school facilities to produce a more varied programme.

In the school, Bob Aitchison, now one of the assistant headteachers, had organised a small number of adult classes. These were the seeds of the new Craigroyston Community High School. These first few adults seeking a second chance at education spurred us on to find a way to change Craigie into a community school. It appeared an insurmountable task. Lothian Region was not interested, since, at the time, it was too involved in opening its first group of purpose-built community schools. It did not recognise that the essence of a community school was what went on inside it rather than a showpiece of design. In other words, the model should be education-led not architecture-led.

In the summer term of 1979 I was playing golf at Killermont with a headteacher friend from a Glasgow secondary school. In the course of the round he mentioned that Strathclyde Region Education Committee had made an approach to an international foundation for an injection of money to be used towards educational innovation. He would not give me any more concrete information, because the councillors on the Education Committee could not agree which schools should get the injection of extra money. Each wanted it for his or her own area. After some leg-pulling, my friend agreed that the booklet about the foundation should be the side-bet of our match. This was a prospect I did not wholly relish, as he was the better golfer. However, nothing ventured... Since August 1972 I had slept, eaten and worried about Craigie, now I was playing golf for it! My luck held. I won the booklet with information about the Bernard van Leer Foundation based in The Hague. This was a much more valuable prize than the usual fiver.

Bernard van Leer was a Dutch philanthropist who established an educational foundation with the millions his multi-national company had made in packaging and, in particular, from his patent for the valves on oil drums. The foundation is a world-wide organisation, with offices in those countries which has branches of the parent packaging company. Its main aim is to help develop educational initiatives in under-privileged communities in the Western and Third Worlds. These initiatives are aimed at encouraging self-reliance and compensating for negative environments. The proven successes can be replicated elsewhere. Developing a community school in Pilton seemed to fit these criteria. A hurriedly produced draft proposal was forwarded to the Bernard van Leer Foundation.

In the early days of the Craigroyston Trust Fund, applications had been sent to numerous trusts which might be sympathetic. The successful grants were banked and used to underwrite the aims of the school. The proposal forwarded to The Hague simply followed this pattern. If the school received a grant, it would be banked and used to convert Craigie into a community school.

However, it was not as simple as this. The reply from the Bernard van Leer Foundation came after the summer break. It indicated a strong interest in the

107

proposed project but required a detailed proposal, with aims, objectives, costs and a plan to evaluate the project. In order that the staff were part of the new development, a group representative of the breadth of the thinking within the school went to work. Wallace Wood, Isobel Leckie, Billie Smith, Roy Crichton, Ken MacAskill and myself produced the required document for the autumn meeting of the trustees. We had no real idea of the work involved in the project. The success of the earlier CSE project gave everybody the confidence that the switch to a community school could be made in the same way and at the same speed. The staff now knew they were a group of professionals capable of such a development.

To everyone's delight Craigie was offered, in January 1980, a three-year project funded by a £250,000 grant from the Bernard van Leer Foundation, provided there was support from the SED and Lothian Region. Here was a hurdle. To date, Lothian's director of education had not been informed of the proposal. Knowing that the directors had their own association, he might have felt morally obliged to block our move because of its possible negative effect on Strathclyde's forthcoming application.

The director was now in a corner. If he did not support the Craigie initiative, £250,000 would be lost to Lothian. He backed us, albeit reluctantly. An additional offer was made by Lothian Region to allow the school free access to regional services, such as architectural, financial and administrative, which were not covered by the Bernard van Leer Foundation. The project was programmed to start in January 1981.

The euphoria of the grant award was soon diminished when the news broke in the local press. Community groups thought that the school held a pot of gold for distribution to the community. We were inundated with requests of all types. Even the local Women's Guild wrote requesting a new china tea set.

To clear the air and prevent community groups from becoming disillusioned with the school, it was decided to call a meeting of all local professional workers. The aim of the meeting was to clarify the fact that the money was to allow Craigie to evolve into a community school and that it was not a local pump-priming fund. The staff representatives at the meeting were shaken by the reception from some of their fellow professionals. One group wanted the money sent back, because, they argued, Craigie was Lothian's responsibility, and therefore the Region should fund the project. Quite why they argued this I never knew for sure, but I suspected that certain individuals had hidden political agendas which did not include a successful Craigie. It took the persuasion of a local minister, the Reverend Tom Gordon to negotiate a mutual agreement. Any money pumped into Pilton could only do good.

The enormity of the task ahead was beginning to dawn on some of the Craigie staff. To operate a community school required a more gradual approach than that of creating the Craigie Curriculum. However, Craigie's friendly, non-authoritarian atmosphere and a staff which had already coped successfully with innovation proved a fertile seed bed for the Craigroyston Curriculum Project (CCP), the official name for our new venture with the Bernard van Leer Foundation.

The major task facing the CCP was attracting the adult community which had previously been failed by the education system. Why re-enter a system which produced such memories of failure? Why take the long walk from the school gate to the school front door in order to go into an alien institution which might reinforce the past?

The conception of the time-scale of the project was based on our earlier success with curriculum changes. This time, the staff learned the hard way, by trial and error. The CCP increased everybody's workload, but none more so than the school office staff, who had to deal with the increased administration and develop reception skills to cope with the potential adult clients.

The job of Craigie's administrative assistant, Pamela Aitchison, increased and changed. Without her willingness to go the extra mile, the adult programme, the renting of school property and the hiring of minibuses would never have been so successful. As more cash came into the school, her job became that of a bursar. It took years, however, to have the Region acknowledge this with a post upgrading. A bureaucracy can never adapt quickly. Rules are sacred.

However, Craigie's friendly atmosphere encouraged the adults to enrol. Many hours of the staff in-service programme were devoted to the community aspect of the school. The working parties controlling each of the integral parts of the CCP comprised a carefully planned mixture of staff and community activists, which proved to be a learning experience for both groups.

It gradually became apparent that there was a flaw in the original work plan, in that it lacked a community-education dimension. The cost of a community educator was not included in the proposal because everybody had assumed that the staff could do the work involved. George Rubienski was appointed to the post of assistant head community affairs, and after a great deal of work both of us, independently, realised that a successful adult-education programme required staff trained in teaching adults.

An interesting experience for staff was working with the adults who were not interested in exam-based courses but rather learning for the sake of learning. We found that the short courses, in direct contrast to the SCE courses, were more popular. By nature of their length there was no delayed gratification. This, in turn, prepared the ground for the future Scotvec courses.

Many of Craigie's characteristics were conducive to the change-over. The banning of corporal punishment eliminated the chance of there being a double set of standards for adults and students. The removal of the bells was based on the assumption that most people have watches and can read the time. The switching off of the bells happened without fuss. One day the bells were switched off for servicing, and I instructed the head janitor to leave them off for ever. The lack of bells reduced the Victorian factory atmosphere and so removed another point of conflict between staff and students.

The introduction of passing time did the same. This American idea was based on the premise that no one can be in two places at the same time. It is physically impossible for a lesson to finish and the next to start simultaneously. The five minutes between classes gave everyone a break and further enhanced the calmer environment. The staff welcomed both these changes. More importantly, the lack of school rules made Craigie less like the schools the adults had previously disliked. We were forging new ground here. We were way ahead. Indeed many years later, the first question of a visiting

111

headteacher interested in community schooling was, 'What are the adult rules and how do you enforce them?'

Crucial to the success of the project were innovations, such as the Under-Fives Centre (Craigie's version of a nursery), the action-research time required by the foundation, the adult-learning programme and an adult lounge. The lounge, which was to become the focal point for adults using Craigie, was an old classroom. I persuaded a national building company which was currently upgrading and privatising some of the rundown local council houses to fund the conversion, decoration and furnishing of the lounge. Bluntly asking companies working in the area for money in the form of labour was a technique I frequently used to upgrade Craigie when local-authority funds were unavailable. The lounge was handed over to the adults, who controlled its use through their own organisation, Craigroyston Adult Students Association. The school could only use the lounge with the consent of CASA. The staff were concerned about drug-users in the building while students were present, and they brokered an agreement with CASA that no one could use the school facilities while under the influence.

Gradually the number of adults grew, at first in recreational classes but soon in vocational and academic classes. Although many adults attended adult-only classes, taught by staff or hired-in community-education tutors, they also attended mainstream classes with the senior students. The age-groups mixed well, to such an extent that the adults invited the students to use their lounge and cafeteria at the breaks. The invitation was nearly always declined because of the smoky atmosphere.

The adults in the mainstream classes acted as a

calming influence and thereby increased the work-rate of the students. These adults were volunteers and wanted to learn. This point clearly underlines Neill's view that people learn rapidly when they are motivated. The only complaint that ever percolated through to me was that the students objected to the adults 'hogging the teachers' time by asking questions and demanding attention'. Some interesting situations developed in this new educational environment. One amusing role-reversal occurred when a boy wrote an absence note for his father who was too ill to attend his classes. An early English class actually contained a mother and daughter. The former was delighted when she gained better grades in the SCE examination than her offspring. There were many successes. Local people entered university and college. The mother of one of our students became involved in a writing scheme. This led to her writing a play which was successfully produced at Edinburgh's Traverse Theatre.

Rab Purves, Richard White and Maldwyn Stride successfully attracted many adults to their diverse range of art classes. In keeping with the Craigie Curriculum, they set up an annual residential art weekend at Hospitalfield, near Arbroath, which included both adult and teenage students. One adult student made it to art college, joining a group of young Craigie artists who had already gone there. This talented group produced enough quality work to allow me to persuade the City of Edinburgh Art Centre to mount an exhibition, *After Images*, which ran from December 1985 to February 1986. Many of the works of art were sold, but, more importantly, the exhibition was a clear recognition of the talent of these young working-class Scots who could so easily be overlooked in an authoritarian educational system.

113

Much more important were the adults who gained in self-esteem and confidence as the feeling developed that they had something to offer to society. Anybody interested in developing community schooling should remember that the most important achievement is making people feel good about themselves. Everything else is secondary. It was certainly true at Craigie, where we had pursued the same formula with the students.

Although I was director of the CCP and Wallace Wood was the co-ordinator, there was a management committee made up of teachers and local people. This was an attempt to democratise the decision-making process, and it was reasonably successful. The main problem area was the annual budget meeting, which produced arguments over the division of the grant.

Naturally, there was never enough money to satisfy all the demands from the various working parties. At one time, the local activists from certain working parties, ably assisted by the evaluators, wanted the total grant handed over to them, in order that they could divide it up according to their own priorities. At the same time Craigie would be left administering the CCP, reporting to the foundation and ensuring that money kept arriving. The staff on the management committee, including myself, had to defend the interests of the students. We agreed that they were part of the community and the essential core of the community school.

This argument won the day, so the whole-school-based aspects of the CCP – the resource centre, the residential programme's subsidy and School House Primary Unit – continued to receive their fair share of the monies.

The original plan attacked the problem of communication head on. It was clear that in Pilton a percentage of the population was totally handicapped by their functional illiteracy and innumeracy. This disadvantage made it difficult for them to have a meaningful dialogue with local and national bureaucracies. In order to help combat this problem, the posts of a communication skills worker, specialising in video work, an adult basic educator and a local historian were included in the original submission. Craigie's school magazine was converted into the local free newspaper the *North Edinburgh News*, thus emphasising the importance of communication.

During Session 1988–89, the last year of the CCP, there was a great deal of worry about the future of the embryonic community school. It became obvious that Lothian Region was not yet in a position to mainstream the project. The foundation made it clear that it was prepared to consider a second phase of funding. This grant would wean Craigie away from the foundation and give us time to pressurise Lothian Region into creating its first non-purpose-built community school.

CHAPTER SIXTEEN

Enter the Little People

The Under-Fives Centre started its life in a cupboard. It was initially staffed by two excellent members of Lothian's nursery service, Wendy Dignan, a nursery teacher, and Grace Anderson, a nursery nurse, whose understanding of the work resulted in the centre becoming the linchpin of the Craigroyston Curriculum Project.

The centre was soon moved to a vacant, but specially adapted, space in the music block, where it developed its three-pronged philosophy: to educate and socialise the infants; to give the parents a second chance at education; and to enhance and develop the parenting skills of the adults, who were mainly single-parent mothers.

The centre moved away from the traditional nursery model into areas related to its three-pronged philosophy involving the children's education, the parents' education and the joint education of both child and parent. The first point of difference was that the children's attendance was normally restricted to times when the parents were attending classes. This meant that in a week the number of children attending could be as high as 70, but the pattern was related to their parents' classes in Craigie. The centre was not designed to allow parents the freedom to work, but solely as an educational tool that allowed them access to education. Parental involvement in the child's education was intended to be a confidence-building strategy. Most parents saw themselves as failures, caught in the poverty trap, with the result that they had very low self-esteem. The programme in the Under-Fives Centre, plus the educational activities in Craigie, were designed to combat this. Over the years, success was measured by the number of women whose life took on new impetus and new meaning. It was wonderful to see these 'born-again' human beings. It also emphasised the importance of the parent in the child's development and education. This was unusual. In most schools, the professionals exclude parents from the educational process. This demystification of education was possibly the most important confidence-building strategy. I always found great pleasure in visiting the centre and watching the parents and children at play. The atmosphere of pleasure and joy was one Neill would have revelled in.

Being on campus, the centre had easy access to the expertise and facilities of the secondary school's departments. This resulted in the development of a broad-based adult programme, which reflected many of the features of Craigie's mainstream programme. It included, for example, outdoor education for the mothers and children. The school was back to the Queen's Park outdoor education beginnings – and this time the parents were not surrogate.

Craigie students also helped. Much of the furniture

and toys were made in the technical department by school-age students in the CSE Mode 3 technology course. The student mums were also involved – a delightful toy telephone kiosk was made by one mum as a farewell gift.

The research work of Joyce Watt, of Aberdeen University, on the centre clearly illustrates the importance it played in the lives of the mothers. 'It's a life-saver – I needed contact with other adults' and 'I think I'm a more interesting person now – and I'm sure I'm a better mother' were two of the responses she canvassed.

The warm and welcoming atmosphere of the centre complemented that of the main building. The children were never out of place in the school corridors. The natural exuberance of toddlers was a part of life in the dining-hall. When I met Grace in the corridor with a group of toddlers she always explained to them that I was Hugh, who ran their school. Another facet of Craigie's Neillian nature was Grace herself. She was a Neillian by nature. Her attitudes were instinctive rather than learned.

Students on the CSE child-care course were often on placement in the centre. This was another attempt to break the cycle that handicaps estates like Pilton. Many students were skilled at looking after younger siblings in the family situation and at this stage in their lives had a very warm and positive attitude towards young children. The nurturing of this warmth allowed the students an opportunity to practise parenting skills, in advance of becoming parents themselves, and afforded them an insight into toddlerhood in a loving environment.

The centre's success resulted in a number of problems which required a limited entrance policy. Only parents wishing to attend Craigie's adult programme could use the centre. It also had to be limited to parents living in the school catchment area. The latter restriction was necessary to prevent its being taken over by middle-class parents living in the neighbourhoods close to Pilton. This group, which was adept at recognising an excellent free facility, had vigorously campaigned in the early 1970s against the inclusion of their homes in Craigroyston's catchment area. At the time of reorganisation, the campaign in the press had been vicious. 'I would not send my dog, far less my children, to Craigroyston' ran a letter in the *Scotsman* in October 1976.

The campaign had, of course, been successful – any other outcome in this class-torn city would have been miraculous. Our refusal to allow entry to parents from the areas which had campaigned against Craigroyston was not revenge. We simply felt that we should serve our catchment area and that it was unlikely that any under-five from outwith the Pilton area would become a Craigie student in later life.

The centre's progress is well documented in all the Craigroyston Curriculum Project's reports to the Bernard van Leer Foundation, the evaluation documents and the research of Joyce Watts, who wrote, 'The Under-Fives Centre in Craigroyston High School is uniquely placed to contribute to what will be a long-term debate about the community role in pre-school, in general, and nursery education in particular.'

The centre also featured in national television programmes on nursery education as an example of excellence.

The research reflected the Bernard van Leer Foundation's switch in policy from general educational projects to those involved in the development of the pre-fives and their parents. As the centre developed, it was extended to include a library and its own parents' room. The library was a gift from Craigie's most famous former pupil, the footballer Gordon Strachan of Dundee, Aberdeen, Manchester United, Leeds, and Scotland fame. As he sat at a desk in the Under-Fives Centre, writing the cheque, Bob Aitchison was heard to comment that it was the first time in Gordon's life he had furniture which fitted him! The parents' room was virtually home made. It was decorated and furnished by a group of mothers who renovated furniture that had become redundant in the main school.

As the mothers grew in confidence there was a proposal to begin an Open University course in child-care. This proved to be a successful venture and another exciting Craigie first. How the expectations of people change with a rise in self-esteem! If I had suggested at the start of the project that adults from Pilton could have tackled an Open University course, I would have been quietly led off to the 'funny farm'.

Although there were changes in personnel – Chris McCormick took over from Wendy, and Addie Campbell was employed as a nursery assistant – there was no change in the basic philosophy, a fact acknowledged by Grace when she congratulated me on these appointments.

Like earlier Craigie innovations the centre attracted many visitors and became focal to the development of the community school. This became clear during the negotiations with the foundation for second-phase funding. Fraser Henderson, then assistant director of education, and I visited The Hague to present the work plan and budget from the project's directorate and management committee. During our final discussions with Dr W. Welling, the director of the foundation, Fraser was presenting the case in a very low-key manner. The debate was going round in circles. I intervened by pushing across the desk to Dr Welling a folio of photographs taken in the centre. He flicked through the photographs, pressed his buzzer and muttered a few words. His secretary came in with a tray, three glasses and a bottle of Scotch whisky. The photos had done the trick.

The Under-Fives Centre was the engine which pulled Craigie into its second-phase funding.

CHAPTER SEVENTEEN

Craigie Adds the Fifth C

The second phase of the Bernard van Leer funding was used for consolidation. It allowed Craigie to be weaned away from the foundation's funding to become Lothian Region's first non-purpose-built community school.

The major change was the introduction of a community educator, Ian Black, into Craigie. The introduction of an adult-education expert eradicated what had been identified as the main flaw of the first phase. Ian and his successor, Ian Cooke, provided the school with an expertise in working with adults and community groups, an aspect of education which was not part of the training of mainstream teachers. Each of the Ians emphasised the essence of community-education philosophy. An individual adult develops at his or her own rate and makes his or her own decision about learning. I liked this, as it is very close to the philosophy of Neill. Both individuals helped push Craigie along the path to community-school status. They helped to create the community education department, which gave their work equal status with the other departments. Their development of the summer-holiday programme was a major contribution to the Craigie Curriculum and a further opening up of the school to its community.

Ian Cooke's part-time secondment to the Pilton Project, an EC anti-poverty project, produced very close links with Craigie, which partially financed several projects designed to help the whole community. The best examples were a school-based careers office, a series of Scotvec business-studies courses for unemployed adults and help with the European trip.

Ian Cooke was also a member of the senior staff team, giving that group an extra dimension in running a community school. In my opinion, no community school can be run efficiently without a community educator in the senior team.

An interesting development at this stage was the return of our adult students as working members of the school staff. The first para-professional members of staff were two community liaison workers. These two appointments were the start of Craigie's locally recruited para-professional workforce, which was crucial in underscoring the point that local people had indeed something to contribute to the development of their own community school.

Another para-professional, whose children were former students, volunteered to help with the subsidised breakfast programme which ran before school started. This was a welcome innovation for many students who enjoyed this addition to their school day. Unfortunately, the need for this was another indicator that social problems were on the increase. The educational cutbacks caused the subsidies to be removed, with a resultant reduction in Craigie breakfasters. For some of the students, breakfast was essential to improving their work-rate.

The switch in staffing towards community educators, community tutors and para-professionals was the beginning of a trend brought about by the reduction in the roll of school-age students and an increase in the number of adult students. Even with this change in numbers, the statutory school was still the core operation, without which there would be no infrastructure to develop a community school. Staff were now more confident that the adult programme had no detrimental effect on the students, but rather complemented the education of the young people. This became a more significant trend during the Thatcher attack on state education, cunningly disguised as the Parents' Charter.

The successes of the various working parties were for the most part incorporated into the community school. However, two of the groups decided, in my opinion correctly, that it was the right time to branch out on their own. A community school can support community ventures, but they must, at some point, become free-standing organisations. The *North Edinburgh News* became a self-sufficient community newspaper. It later devoted space in every issue to Craigie news, produced and written by students as part of their English studies. Video in Pilton became completely independent, although still based in a flat in School House.

Meanwhile, the clientele of the adult programme had altered in two ways. There was a global increase in numbers and, within this, an increase in the number of male students. There was also a reduction in those who used the adult lounge solely as a social centre. This reflected the fact that the community no longer thought it strange to return to a system which had earlier pronounced it a failure.

At the finish of the Craigroyston Curriculum Project the financial support from Bernard van Leer came to an end but Craigie still remained a member of the Bernard van Leer family. Contact was maintained through the foundation's publicity machine, but, more importantly, through the development of the Scottish Network of Bernard van Leer sponsored projects.

Since the start of the Craigroyston Curriculum Project three other projects, all aimed at the educational trilogy of Craigie's Under-Fives Centre – the under-fives themselves, their parents and the education of both – had begun. The Partnership in Education project was situated in Priesthill, a Glasgow council estate similar to Pilton. Young Families Now! was in Torry, Aberdeen, another underprivileged community, and Guth nam Parant was in the Western Isles.

Chris McCormick and I became involved in networking with the staff of the other three projects. The original aim was to develop in-service training for the staff of all four projects, sponsored by the Bernard van Leer Foundation. At one such session it was agreed to invite parents from each project to visit the International Children's Festival, held in Edinburgh each May. Although Craigroyston's Under-Fives Centre would play host, the difference in the idea was that the parents would organise their own visit.

The success of the visit generated the idea that the following year's visit to the Festival would include the infants. Although sponsored by Bernard van Leer, the visit was again organised by the parents, proof that people can and will rise to a challenge. The parents had never tackled anything like this before. The success of the event was further evidence of Neill's view that people can develop when they are given the opportunity. Once again, it was a pleasure to see adults grow in stature – the philosophy of the Under-Fives Centre was being applied on a national basis.

All the projects are now complete but the Bernard van Leer Foundation funds the Scottish Network – Family Policy Resources Unit at Caledonian University, Glasgow. The unit, under the directorship of Peter Lee, from the Glasgow project, hopes to continue the work of the four projects, influencing local political decision-makers and the multifarious charities who are working in the field of early education. This is surely the age-group to invest in if society really wishes to break the cycle of deprivation.

As the Van Leer Foundation funding was phased out for Craigie, a great deal of time and energy was spent persuading Lothian Region's politicians and officials to grant Craigie community-school status. Our case was based on the successes of the Craigroyston Curriculum Project, the further opening up of the school to the neighbourhood, the summer-holiday programme, the Under-Fives Centre, the adult programme and the development of the community-education ethos. This was packaged as a model for a non-purpose-built community school in sharp contrast to the Region's more expensive version – a purpose-built community school.

The difference between these two models is that the former is a building gradually converted to community use. The specific conversions reflect the needs and aspirations of the community in the school. The latter has been planned round the perceived needs of the community, and when completed imposed on it. People then have to adapt to the ideas of the planner and the architects.

The purpose-built model is also more expensive. It is profession-led as opposed to the other, which is people or community-led. The latter acknowledges that a community has something to offer its own educational process and is an adult extension of Neill's philosophy.

This financial aspect was vital because of the shift in the economic climate from the easy-spending 1970s to the tight economics of the 1980s. The policies of the market-place had begun to infiltrate education. I was convinced that the non-purpose-built model was the right way forward for the community-school movement. Existing schools could be modified to cope with their community aspirations.

The lobby was successful partly because of the success of the Craigroyston Curriculum Project and partly because other schools, such as Drummond High School and Balerno High School, had joined Craigroyston in the community-school campaign.

Both these schools had decided, independently, that they wished to serve their communities in a fuller way and had applied for community-school status. This extra pressure no doubt helped our case with Lothian Region, which was hesitating because of government financial restrictions. On 18 January 1985, Craigie was granted community-school status. The long haul from junior-secondary days was complete.

This, however, led to a further financial problem. All Lothian's community schools had to generate their income from adult class fees. This was less of a problem for the other two new community schools, given the nature of their catchment areas. It would prove a nightmare for Craigie. At the bank one day, a thought struck me. If a bank card gave access to money, could a similar piece of plastic not do the same for education? The idea of an education key card was born. For a single payment an adult student could purchase an education card, which provided access to as many classes as he or she could possibly attend during the session for which the card was valid. The initial payment was heavily discounted for local residents, OAPs, holders of UB40s and those on Social Security. For adults outwith the catchment area the fee would be higher.

To my astonishment this proposal was approved by the Education Committee, allowing the adults access to second-chance education. No extra funding was provided for administration, however, and as the key card allowed access to education for so many people, it produced an even heavier load on the office staff and the para-professionals. Although the key-card system was a remarkable breakthrough, it irritated me that such a solution was necessary. I feel strongly that people should be entitled to free education when they are ready for it. The notion that education for the bulk of the population should finish at 16 is an out-dated reflection of the needs of Victorian industrial society. People should have free access to education at the point they choose it to improve their quality of life.

The experience gained during the Craigroyston Curriculum Project was recognised in 1990, when I was very fortunate to be granted a sabbatical term at Edinburgh University under the auspices of the Robert Reid Fellowship. This allowed me time to think and reflect on

Craigie's status as a community school. This time out was precious because being involved in day-to-day education leaves little time for thought. I decided to visit and study community schools in both the UK and the USA. The results of this study convinced me that the Craigie model of an integrated non-purpose-built school was the correct one for the future. Very few, if any, purpose-built community schools would be constructed in the future, for two reasons. Firstly, there were financial restrictions, but secondly, and interestingly, thinking had switched from imposing a model on a community to allowing a model reflecting the community's aspirations to emerge. My paper was accepted by Lothian Region as the basis of future development. This was yet another compliment to the teaching and non-teaching staff of Craigie, who had helped develop the working model in the year of the Craigroyston Curriculum Project. The fifth C, community consciousness, now took its place beside the original four.

CHAPTER EIGHTEEN

The Heidie Goes to Court

The Conservative government's attempt to control the teaching profession took the form of a policy that operated on a number of fronts. There was an attack on salaries, the introduction of teacher appraisal and a move towards greater control over the curriculum. In Scotland, the salaries aspect produced the Teachers' Action, which was a direct challenge to the government's pay offer, and which many people have considered to be one of the few successful trade-union actions in the Thatcher years. The influence of the campaign, which lasted from 1984–86, affected the whole country. The rolling programme of strikes and the withdrawal from all non-curricular activities had a dramatic effect on Craigie's de-schooling policies. There was almost total staff support for the campaign. One assistant headteacher, George Rubienski, because of his position in the EIS, played an important role in the national campaign.

As both a staff member and an EIS member, I agreed with the broad plan of action because, if success-

130

ful, it would lead to improved conditions for the under-paid younger members of the profession. I disagreed, however, on two points. I continued to supervise the students while they ate their lunch because I was convinced that school lunches played a vital part in the diet of many of Craigie's students. Secondly, the field trips had been an integral part of the curriculum, but the EIS took the view that they were extra-curricular. The staff supported the EIS position, and, reluctantly, I had to accept the majority view. No field trips ran in 1985.

As the session and the action progressed, an issue developed around those teachers who would not co-operate with the Scottish Examination Board procedures for the administration of the national exams. The EIS instructed its members to refuse to do the clerical work necessary for the smooth running of the Ordinary and Higher Grade exams. The directors of education in Scotland responded in various ways. In Lothian, the director asked the headteachers for the names of non-co-operating staff members. I refused to comply with the director's instructions. Suddenly I found myself, in the company of 11 other heads, at the epicentre of a major row. After three months of pressure from the Region, only four heads still held out against the dictat. Further tail-twisting reduced the number to three. Each of us was separately interviewed by the directorate and given 24 hours to comply, or face loss of salary.

When the phone-call came from the director 24 hours later, I still refused to divulge the names, and my salary was withdrawn immediately. The reaction of the other Craigie EIS staff was instant. They went on strike while I continued to work on my own, without salary. My long-held belief that the headteacher is simply a

131

member of staff, with a different function, had been validated in the most difficult of circumstances.

The issue was resolved by the EIS. They advised me to take out an injunction against the Region to prevent them from arresting my salary. I did so. The Region backed down at the eleventh hour. I was actually instructing my counsel at the High Court when we were informed of the Region's U-turn.

The next day, Saturday, I found myself, along with Henry Philip, headteacher of Liberton High in Edinburgh, invited by John Pollock, the EIS general secretary, to head the EIS national protest march along Princes Street. I felt this action was a fitting conclusion to a hair-raising period in my life, and it strengthened my view of what the headteacher's relationship with the teaching staff should be. One of the negative effects of the strike action was the departure of most Scottish headteachers from the EIS. This indicated a 'them-and-us' situation which fitted the management techniques of the business world which were being imposed on schools by the Thatcher government.

CHAPTER NINETEEN

Brochures, Budgets and Bureaucracy

The granting of community-school status had a sting in its tail: there was to be no extra payment to staff for the extra work and no increase in the school's capitation allowance to reflect the adult numbers. This was the sharp end of the free-market economy, with its accountants' attitude to the world of education.

The extra work was to be carried out by the time-honoured method of staff goodwill, a fact actually minuted by the Education Committee when they granted Craigie community-school status. Such typically British amateurism was no longer acceptable to teachers and finally disappeared during the teachers' action. The machinery of the 'Thatcher Revolution' was being forced on to state education, cleverly disguised under the populist banner of the Parents' Charter. The charter claimed to give all parents the right to send their offspring to the school of their choice. On the surface, this seems an obvious democratic right, and in isolation it might have been harmless, but, when linked to the other facets of Conservative education policy, it became lethal. It was quite simply intended to destroy the comprehensive system and undermine an articulate teaching profession that was perceived by the government as predominantly left of centre.

This political drive was clearly recognised by the local councillor, Neil Lindsay, who had sent his two children to Craigie. At a School Council meeting, he stated that the Parents' Charter was, in his view, a carefully constructed long-term covert strategy to destroy the comprehensive system. He saw the Parents' Charter as a lethal cocktail whose ingredients were renewed support for the private sector, creation of school boards, a national curriculum, devolved school management, national testing, staff appraisal and league tables of examination results and truancy rates. This cleverly constructed plan negated much of the progress made by the comprehensive system. In this way the system was discredited before it had adequate time to produce its intended result of creating a more fulfilled young population.

The attempt to control the profession was motivated by the claim that it was mainly comprised of a 'bunch of lefties', who were poisoning the minds of future voters. In Scotland, the lack of a Conservative majority and Labour's control of most local authorities produced some resistance to these policies. Various campaigns were led by the teachers' unions, in particular the EIS, by parents' organisations and, on occasion, by a fusion of teachers and parents.

Policies were dictated by the profit motive. The care and development of young people was not important. At this time many of the headteacher's in-service sessions were devoted to integrating business techniques into schools. The lecturers, from the business sector, naturally saw everything in terms of profit and loss. This they translated into examination results, without any social or ability weighting related to the school's population. I remember at one such session trying to explain that in their simplistic terms Craigie was already bankrupt, and therefore their approach was nonsense, but this was lost on the money men. The profit-and-loss school of educational thinking was the forerunner to the government's imposition of league tables of examination results, which year after year placed Craigie, in football terms, in the relegation zone. With nowhere to be relegated to, there developed the beginning of the feeling that school closure was the educational equivalent of no-man's land.

How do you measure work carried out with damaged children? If tables had been produced on guidance time spent with individual students, Craigie might well have come out on top. In their present form league tables are a nonsense, a point underlined by Sir Claus Mauser, a retired government statistician. In his speech at the Jerwood Award Ceremony in November 1992, he said that, in his opinion, league tables are inherently dishonest. By their weighting of certain aspects of education over others, they would always belittle some hard-working schools. Neill's measure of success would certainly not include statistics. He based success on the development of happy individuals, who would make a positive contribution to their society in the future.

The other method by which the government identified successful schools was measurement of truancy rates. Again, there was no weighting for social problems

135

facing young people. Many students arrived late at Craigie, having had to cope with staggering problems which might have kept away from school many of the adults teaching them. My early technique of standing at the front door was a welcoming gesture. The old adage 'better late than never' certainly applied to Craigie. The staff knew only too well that for some students coming to school was more comforting than being at home.

Nevertheless, in government terms we were failing. Thatcher's policies declared Craigie bankrupt and a failure. The school was placed firmly in the relegation zone of the two new education leagues. We had turned full cycle within the state sector. Once again Craigroyston was being measured against the private sector. In business terms we should have locked the front door and thrown away the keys. Educationally, of course, this would be nonsense. A community without a school is untenable. Its very heart would be silenced. But government policies were not concerned with moral or educational ideals, simply with money.

While everything we were doing was being brutally hacked up in an Orwellian double-think *coup de grâce*, Craigie was nominated for and gained a Curriculum Award in 1984 and again in 1987. This award, comparable to the Queen's Award for Industry, is given to UK schools working for and with their communities. A school functioning at the heart of its community seemed a less competitive way to evaluate success. The community-school movement was clearly pointing a way forward to any politician able to read the runes. The two awards and the school's development plan, Craigie 2000, gave further impetus. The best way to combat the Tories' attacks would be to keep moving forward.

Looking back, a major mistake was not pressurising local politicians to make it more difficult for parents to choose other schools when the Parents' Charter was implemented in Lothian. A publicity drive about local schools might have halted the drift to the more famous schools at Craigie's expense.

Like all schools in Scotland's peripheral housing estates, Craigie was adversely affected by the government's attack. The destructive effect of the Conservative policies was exacerbated by the demographic change in the school's catchment area. The parents of the 1950s and 1960s had become senior citizens, and the children had moved away. It was also affected by the refurbishment and sale of council houses in West Pilton – yet another government attack on working-class housing estates. This produced the emergence of an underclass in the area, as the government developed their new two-tier approach to education, the Health Service and the multifarious problems covered by the social services. The government's aim seemed to be to provide a superior service, at a cost, for those with money and an inferior state-run service for the lower-income groups. Any doubts about the appearance of an underclass were removed when Pilton became one of the four areas in the UK (one other was Toxteth, Liverpool) to be included in the Third European Community Anti-Poverty Programme in 1991, which led to another injection of money into the area.

The demographic changes meant there was now room in many of Edinburgh's more historically famous schools. Applications for places in these schools rose alarmingly. The Edinburgh Question had reappeared! This, allied to the social aspirations of those people buying the West Pilton council houses, caused the number of Craigie students to plummet. The result of this was the transfer of staff, most of whom would have preferred to stay at Craigie. While this was a very painful time, it was heartening that many staff demonstrated their belief in the school by developing effective techniques for failing their transfer interviews: outrageous hairstyles, denim clothing and bikers' leathers frightened off many a traditional headteacher. In marked contrast with the staff loyalty to the aims of the school was the action of a few of the successful adult students, who used Craigie's pioneering adult-education programme but sent their children to study elsewhere.

As student numbers declined, adult numbers rose and there was always a waiting list for the Under-Fives Centre. This served to underline the importance of community-school status, however underfunded. By 1990 the problem of declining school rolls in Lothian had reached the point where there was government financial pressure to produce a policy of school closures. To my horror, the closure of Craigie became a possibility.

The proposed closure produced an outburst of energy from both the school and the community. In many respects this was very reassuring, for all of us on the staff were unaware of the high esteem in which the school was held by the community. Even some of the activists who had been antagonistic in other circumstances were now supportive. Quickly a Save Craigie campaign was started, fronted by the School Board and supported by the management committee of the community centre. A document, Craigie 2000, was produced to focus the campaign. This document contained a development plan, laying out the future of the school. This was vital. The plan was forward looking and maintained the momentum and energy that had prevented Craigie from stultifying in the past. The campaign was successful. Craigie stayed open, and the development plan was implemented.

The reduction in student numbers had one advantage – space in the form of empty classrooms in the only large building in West Pilton. Community organisations with inadequate or unsuitable accommodation opened up discussions as to the possibility of renting space in Craigie. There were two plusses in this. The organisations provided money for the community-school operation but, much more important, the community actually asked to come into Craigie. This further reduction in alienation was achieved without diluting the ethos of the school. In all the negotiations with the various groups, it was made absolutely clear that they would be in a school and the students were its core. Rules and restrictions would not be introduced to please the outside groups expressing concern about the students exercising the freedom of their building.

Women in a New Direction (WAND), Pilton Opportunity Project (POPS), Link Holidays, Volunteer Tutors and Edinburgh District Council Housing Department all established their projects in Craigie. All these organisations worked with different groups or individuals within the community, so there was a logic to their working in the community school. As the clients of each project visited the school, they were regarded as potential students for the adult programme. This was the best kind of PR for Craigie.

WAND attracted a large number of women who wished to take tentative steps towards starting a new educational career. This led to WAND directing clients to our adult programmes and helping to amend the programme to suit the requirements of their client group. This was another Neillian example of people starting education when they were ready. This second chance at education led to a growing self-respect, confidence and sense of usefulness. It was a 1990s' form of Neill's philosophy and another way of spelling out Craigie's five Cs.

As the numbers declined, the intake changed. There were fewer more able students and a greater proportion of disturbed students from families suffering from the acute stresses of living in the underclass. Most of the staff now had long service in Craigie and were skilled at dealing with difficult children. Nevertheless, the shift in the nature of the intake made the job of the staff significantly harder. New child-centred strategies had to be developed to help ameliorate the problem. The Base was created in the Learning Centre as a 'cooling-off' technique – students could be placed there and continue their classwork under the personal supervision of a timetabled member of staff. I acted as gate-keeper, controlling when a student could go into and leave the Base. Although I took advice from the staff, I held responsibility myself for prioritising those children who most needed help.

A problem facing a small number of students was lack of adequate clothing, especially footwear. This often prevented them from attending school. As with all non-attendance problems, quick action is required to prevent the establishment of a pattern. As a result, the school fund was used to buy clothing for those students who were identified by the guidance staff as having a genuine need. These students were taken shopping by the welfare assistant. This prompt action often resolved the non-attendance problem and circumvented the Region's system, which was slow and bureaucratically cumbersome. The success of our action also removed the necessity for punitive action by the Region. It was a more humane and cheaper solution.

Another child-centred strategy was the Haven. This was a small group of first-year students with problems, which met with one of the guidance staff, Annie Miller, first thing each morning. She provided a friendly ear for our most vulnerable young students. This was yet another example that Craigie cared. The personal touch and the knowledge that they would have an early morning house-call if they failed to reach school was successful.

The Base and the Haven were expensive in staffing but the personal care and the absence of punishment fitted the Neillian model. Children need attention! This fact is conveniently forgotten or ignored in the Thatcherite approach to education. In the Back to Basics drive, there is no understanding that, in a system which has eradicated corporal punishment, guidance time is essential. The link between guidance and examination results is not immediately obvious, with the result that this time spent with children is gradually being cut back and the staff are being asked to use more of their time teaching their original discipline. This reduction is a recipe for disaster. Counselling time is time well spent for the child, his or her classmates, the teachers and the school in general.

A great deal of staff time has been syphoned off into energy-sapping activities, such as producing mission statements, ethos indicators, quality-control factors, workplans and budgets. My guess is that Neill would have used the Scottish word 'daft' to describe these activities, which have built up a paper wall between the students and the staff.

An even sadder effect of the increase in educational jargon, which is now a real growth industry, is the communication barrier it places between staff and parents. As this barrier grows, the profession is being harassed by government to communicate more freely with parents. This development is clearly described by Judith Gillespie in a *Scotsman* article in February 1994 headlined DISMAL FAILURE IN THE SIMPLE ART OF COMMUNICATION.

Craigie, like every other school, suffered from great mental pressure on the profession. From the mid-1980s onwards, Scottish teachers were exposed to constant curricular changes. There was no time to settle. Pressure of work mounted, and the morale of the staff was increasingly undermined. At one point staff felt that not a week passed without a new edict changing, adding to or subtracting from the curriculum model. The pressure on the curriculum and the changes in management techniques diverted a great deal of the energy of the profession away from its primary function. Much paper was generated as evidence that schools had policies. Although I still saw myself as an enabler, a new role of protector emerged. In my view it was imperative to divert or delay these changes as long as possible in order to allow staff time to teach. This was the age of expensive glossy brochures, policy documents, development plans and ever-increasing bureaucracy. The Conservative government claims that it has spent more on education than its predecessor. That may well be so, but the money has not filtered down to the classroom. In all of this there was no mention of, or concern for, children. The fat cats had won the day.

CHAPTER TWENTY

Craigie Visits the European Union

As was so often the case, good ideas began with out-of-school social chats. One Friday evening over a pint of real ale, two other members of staff, Jim MacDonald, Ronnie Kirkham and I were reminiscing about past field trips. Gradually, the conversation drifted to suggestions of a European field trip and we joked about putting the whole school into a jumbo jet and taking Craigie students *en masse* to mainland Europe to celebrate the creation of the European Union in 1992. During the following week I mulled over the idea, and, as I did so, it became less of a joke and more the germ of an educational project. Craigie would have a fresh focus for its curriculum, and it would also provide a memorable experience for the students, many of whom had never been outside Scotland.

At the start of the 1990–91 session, I outlined the project to the staff, who first greeted the idea with a stunned silence and then hysterical laughter. However, it was agreed that the idea should be explored. Many of the staff were attracted by the idea but had reservations – they wanted details about costs, locations and language difficulties. Over the months a small committee and myself worked on various ways forward. We found we were faced with many problems. Apart from a lack of money, I could not find an airline prepared to carry the whole school to a single central continental location.

The committee settled on a four-centre visit for S1, S2, S3 and the seniors. Two centres would be in France and two in Spain, reflecting the staff's linguistic skills and the ease of finding suitable locations. As ever, money was a crucial factor. The mythical European Community 'gravy train' had no cash for such a venture. The Pilton Project promised support. Fraser Henderson, the assistant director, was contacted. He laughingly gave his approval and a promise of support if the project ever got off the ground.

The plan was again presented to the staff. The outline proposal was agreed. Students and their parents were to be informed. We knew that once it was public knowledge we were committed to seeing it through.

We decided that the aims for the visit should be the focus for the year's curriculum. Departments set about finding ways of incorporating Europe '92 into their curriculum. Some departments, such as modern languages, history, geography and maths, had an obvious involvement. Art and media studies produced an award-winning video of the preparations. The PE department agreed to ensure that all taking part in the venture would pass a swimming test. All home economics students made their own toilet bags. I, myself, took on the task of raising the £60,000 required to subsidise the venture. The normal

Craigie rule that no student would be excluded on financial grounds would apply to Europe. Every student who took part received at least a 50 per cent subsidy. Once the project started the enthusiasm grew. Most staff, both teaching and non-teaching, participated. Margaret Blair and Norma Henderson from the school office were a real asset on the S1 trip.

We were allocated to the four excursions – S1 were bound for Tossa De Mar in Spain, S2 to Combrit in the Brittany area of France, S3 to Cala Bona in Majorca and the seniors to Les Biards in Normandy. Prior to departure, the project was given major coverage in the local media, with the result that the idea caught on throughout the city.

Companies, trust funds, individuals, staff friends and even staff all gave generously. Some undertook to sponsor a child or a group of children, hoping that the youngsters would have a memorable experience. The editor of the Edinburgh *Evening News* became interested in the project and sent a reporter and photographer to Les Biards, which resulted in a full-page cover.

We planned that the excursions would follow the normal Craigie residential programme, in that they would be both educational and recreational. As many subjects as possible would be incorporated into the work done on location, and all the students would keep a log of their visit. It would not simply be a holiday.

Because I was able to claim to some pidgin Spanish, I was in charge of S1 at Tossa, where we stayed in a hotel run by Thomson Holidays. As the departure date approached, we all became jittery. Very few students had ever been abroad. Even fewer had been in an aeroplane. We were staying in a hotel with other guests. Would they

145

complain? Not many people would be overjoyed at the arrival in their holiday hotel of a party of sixty 13-year-olds! Would the children, in their excitement, forget what was expected of them and treat the holidaymakers as invisible?

We should have had more faith in the students and their ability to adapt. One incident illustrates this. As I walked past the hotel pool, a holidaymaker stopped and asked me, 'Are you in charge of these kids?' The hair rose on the back of my neck. What disaster had taken place? But, to my delight, he smiled and said, 'Your pupils are a credit to your school. Their behaviour is remarkable and their enjoyment is infectious. Our holiday has been made happier by watching them enjoy themselves.' And thus it was elsewhere. Neill would have been delighted with this pleasure in allowing a child to enjoy the natural expression of freedom in play.

One of the recreational visits was to a local *aqualandia* in Lloret de Mar. I was sitting on the grass watching the students being children at play. It was fascinating to watch 13-year-olds play like eight- or nine-year-olds, underlining the point that children need play as part of their maturing process. While I was observing them, two girls approached me and asked if I would like to go down the water shute. They offered to keep me company, so we spent the next hour on various water shutes as a family group.

In Tossa we varied the activities. Hill-walking in the Montsery Parque Natural, bird-watching in the Aiguamolls de L'Emporda, historical visits, contact with the local school for a football match and a visit to the Dali Museum in Figueras were all on the itinerary.

Dali had clearly made an impression on one girl.

Walking along a country road while bird-watching with a group I heard, 'Sir, sir, did Dali do all these paintings when he was alive?' Two steps later I replied, 'I think so.' Perhaps surrealism had come home to roost at Craigie.

CHAPTER TWENTY-ONE

Reflections

The phone rang. 'Why don't you prepare a submission for the Jerwood Award?' It was Bill Gatherer, the retired former chief adviser for Lothian Region, who had previously persuaded me to enter Craigie for the Curriculum Award. He explained that the Jerwood Award had been established by John Jerwood, a philanthropist who had made his money in the Japanese pearl industry. We discussed his idea. Bill was convinced that Craigie's curriculum innovations over the years would make it a likely candidate for an award. The Jerwood Award was a retrospective award, presented annually to educational institutions or educators who had made a positive contribution to the development of British education. To manage the award, the Jerwood Foundation had been established with a group of prominent individuals as trustees acting as adjudicators. I was hesitant, but the award of a large cash prize stimulated my interest. It certainly would make a significant difference to the Trust Fund. To produce a historical submission about Craigie was going to involve a lot of work, but I agreed, not really expecting a response. None came!

A year later came a similar phone call from Bill, who was still convinced that Craigie's work justified an award. His powers of persuasion, plus my respect for his knowledge of the inner workings of education, produced a second reluctant agreement.

It led to an award of £30,000 for Craigie, in recognition of the school's curriculum achievements over 20 years.

It was obvious that much had been achieved. A former junior secondary had developed into a community high school, and, along the way, it had been a curriculum-development centre for many Scottish schools. This had happened in a catchment area more renowned for its negative publicity than anything else.

Why did it happen? Certainly it is true to say, 'No Neill – no Craigie'. Without my White Waltham meeting with Peter Drewitt, my Craigie career would never have taken place. I had had my share of lucky breaks – Peter, Barnsley and Bernard van Leer – but the driving force was Neill. What would he have made of it all? He certainly would have approved of the non-violent child-centred school, one which successfully attracted its own community, an option not available at Summerhill, a private boarding school. Here was a school with a friendly atmosphere, an atmosphere which always surprised visitors who arrived well versed in the media's negative images of Pilton.

What kept us all going in such a difficult environment? An environment such as this could have easily destroyed the whole thrust of the Craigie Curriculum. Pleasure, enjoyment, nonsense, continual self-driven

149

change and innovation kept the momentum going. The staff over the years became confident of their ability to perform all the tasks that added up to the Craigie Curriculum. Of course, there were moments of doubt, times of lying in bed staring at the ceiling, but there was always someone on the staff willing to share and talk over the problem. Fun was generated in many ways in the school. The annual staff pantomime was a gift to the students at Christmas. The associated fun in planning, writing, casting and costuming took some of the sting out of the long winter term.

The original sponsored event was a 'Womble', named after the TV series of the time. The staff and students were sponsored, by the sackful, to clean the rubbish from the streets and 'back greens' of Pilton. No one can keep an aloof or dignified persona in such an activity. The results were appreciated by the community, and all went well until somebody found a rotting horse's head. The unhygienic nature of the 'Womble' eventually produced a ground-swell among the staff against continuing this type of sponsored event.

After a full debate it was agreed to switch to a sponsored walk. This lacked the community-service element, but the students altered the normal image of a sponsored walk by bringing their dogs, on leads, and siblings, in prams. This always proved to be a day with a high attendance rate. A feature of the event became the participation of the Under-Fives Centre mums with their prams. It had become a whole-school event. Before the 1991 walk, I apologised for the bad weather to two former Craigie students who were back at the centre with their children. 'Don't worry, Hugh,' they said, 'It isn't as bad as our last school walk when you sent us out in the snow.' The dogs on the sponsored walk and the success of the animal-studies course reflected the students' interest in animals.

Pamela Aitchison, the administrative assistant, was a real 'cat lady', who for several years looked after Craigie, the school cat, kindly donated by Joyce, another cat lover. Once the students realised the situation, stray kittens were constantly being brought into the office so that Pamela could find them a good home. This meant I often had kittens wandering about my adjoining office. One day, when I had a beautiful white kitten as a desk ornament, a girl arrived with a note. 'Could Joanna please play with the kitten for a few minutes?' I continued to work while Joanna played with the kitten. When she had finished, she got up from the carpet, said thanks and returned to her class. Was this further proof that animals have a therapeutic effect on children?

A fun day was later added to the calendar of events. Students and staff spent a happy day enjoying all types of funfair games. My own memory is of a mixture of funfair stalls, 'It's a Knock-Out' events, and of students paying money to throw buckets of cold water at me. What a way to make money to subsidise field trips! It was another day when we all met as equals, a process which added to the ever-evolving ethos.

At a later date, when the school population was smaller, a free Christmas lunch was instituted. This was easy in a school where so many of the students were on the free-food roll. Both teaching and non-teaching staff suitably dressed served the meal. I acted as a *maître-d'hôtel* in full black-and-white regalia. The kitchen staff co-operated, even after privatisation.

The staff also tended to form a cohesive social group. In the early years, an Edinburgh pub name appeared on the staff noticeboard each Friday. All of us with a free Friday would gather for a drink and a therapeutic end-of-the-week chat. I often think that the friendships that developed in this way were one of the reasons why I was never seriously attacked at those meetings in which I was pushing the development of the Craigie Curriculum. The *esprit de corps* that developed helped to generate the energy which maintained the momentum, sometimes against the odds as each teacher carried a heavy work-load. For years, Craigie's staff social activities were the talk of the town.

As in many school staffrooms, sport was a great unifier, especially for the men. The football team managed to knock around a few other Edinburgh school staffs and occasionally went on a weekend's tour. The highlight was when I persuaded Bertie Auld, one of the Lisbon Lions, to play for the staff against the students at a farewell game for Cammy Alexander, a fanatical Celtic supporter who was leaving the Craigie staff. Twelve of the staff played for one of Edinburgh's Old Crocks rugby sides. It is difficult to stand on one's dignity in a scrum. The success of the staff golf team led to the inaccurate story that my first question at an interview was, 'What is your golf handicap?' followed by, 'What subject do you teach?'

The innovations followed one another into the Craigie Curriculum. This continuum and the search for improvements prevented the curriculum becoming ossi-fied. The work was accepted because it was school-based, tailor-made for our own students and eventually improved everybody's daily life. This is in direct contrast to the current dispute between the profession and the government, where changes are imposed from outside too rapidly and where there is no obvious improvement in staff working conditions or self-esteem. A government cannot continually denigrate a profession and then expect it to increase its workload. It is difficult to select the most important innovations but CSE Mode 3 and the connection with the Bernard van Leer Foundation probably had most influence on the Craigie Curriculum. There is no question that, for the students, their field trips were the most memorable event of their Craigie life.

There was always pressure, which the staff diffused by social contact and discussion. For me it was more difficult. All the success placed me in a strange position. I was not expected to fail or make a mistake. Although this was never said in so many words, I sensed it. Sometimes, in my own room, I would feel lonely trying to struggle with problems. The solution was just to say to myself, 'What would Neill do in these circumstances?' That often stopped me from making stupid or draconian decisions.

A great deal had been achieved in the way the school was administered and in what was included in the Craigie curriculum. The high-water mark was definitely the late 1970s and early 1980s, when growth was at its maximum, unhampered by the financial cutbacks caused by Tory educational policy and the effects of the recession.

There were also goals not achieved and mistakes made. An organisation has a finite quantity of energy, and aims have to be prioritised, a fact not recognised by the present government. All attempts to establish a students' moot were unsuccessful. The house directors, the people who were to implement this move, did not see it as an important area of their work when they were

153

already struggling to combat the problems of Pilton's growing underclass. Also, the students had no real grasp of what was involved in a meaningful decision-making forum. However, decision-making fora were established among adults in CASA and the senior citizens in the Over-Fifties club.

Work experience never really featured in the Craigie Curriculum, until it was injected via the TVEI initiative. The only exception was a Youth Opportunities Programme established for unemployed ex-students who were given work as teachers' aides in many departments. The technical, science, library, office, audio-visual and janitorial services all gained extra labour, which resulted in training for young people and in giving them the respect that goes with employment. This did not last long. The bureaucrats running the Youth Opportunities Programme read the small print in the legislation and decided that a school was ineligible for financial support.

In the 1970s, specialisation in one aspect of the curriculum, that of developing a centre of excellence, was frowned upon by the teaching 'left' as elitist and therefore inappropriate in the comprehensive system. At that time Julia Carnie had developed an excellent dance group. The students were attracted by the teaching, the rapport and the artistic expression that it allowed. These aspects contributed to successful public performances, which Craigie students normally found difficult when speech was involved. An attempt was made to construct a dance centre, but this idea withered because staff made it clear that they did not approve of a dance school being created within Craigie. Retrospectively, I believe this was a mistake. A dance centre might have attracted students from outwith the catchment area.

In the late 1980s when Craigie was under threat of closure, there was a growing interest in developing features of the curriculum that might attract students from other parts of the city. Stimulus for the idea came from a staff visit to Merksworth in Paisley, where a school in a similar environment had become a centre of hi-tech education. It was all too late! Lothian Region turned down the idea of a centre for computer education at Craigie, placing it in a more socially acceptable area. The official reason given was that the chosen school was close to the city bypass, therefore accessible from all over Lothian.

Although the Education Committee had voted for Craigie to stay open and had supported the school with a generous staffing allowance, which allowed the Craigie Curriculum to flourish (in spite of the Tory cutbacks), it missed the opportunity of making Craigie attractive to other Edinburgh students. The positive-discrimination programme was excellent as far as it was allowed to develop. Both politicians and officials, however, backed away from expensive options, such as the Regional Computer Centre, because of their negative effect on the more traditional schools and the influence of parental pressure. There were two latter-day ideas which never got off the ground. One involved using the students as street wardens, in an attempt to improve the local environment. The students would monitor their own locale for inadequacies in the local authority's services and report them to a central point in Craigie. Secondly, I tried to establish an ex-Craigie student network of marketable skills. The idea was to establish in Craigie an inventory – a Craigie *Yellow Pages* – which would be available to the community and staff. Both ideas were given the thumbs down

155

by the staff. The street-warden scheme would place the students in a vulnerable position. The second idea produced fears about teetering into a 'black-economy network'.

Staff and students being on first-name terms was never a major issue. I adopted a neutral position, and it was left up to the individual teacher to make his or her own decision. Most preferred to maintain a formal arrangement. Willie Wilson was, and continues to be, an outstanding exception, and it worked with no embarrassment to anyone. One day, when Willie was off ill, there was a knock on the staffroom door. I answered it. A student looked me straight in the eye and without any hesitation asked, 'Is Willie back today?' The ethos Willie created within his tutor group was a genuinely family one.

My own relationship with the staff, after the initial period, was close. This was due both to working relationships and friendships developed through social and sporting contacts. This, plus the success of many of our innovations, was mainly positive. Occasionally, at staff meetings, I was placed in a difficult position. On some occasions, I was verbally attacked from the floor by friends. This was hurtful, but I had to absorb it. I decided that losing my temper in public would be counter-productive. Better to absorb the staff anger and reflect in the calm of my office. Usually, I used the managerial technique of doing nothing. This avoided open confrontation with my friends and colleagues. I had, however, the satisfaction of knowing that the staff member who had let off steam was probably feeling better for his or her outburst. I felt sure the friendships were genuine, and arguments were part of the relationship – a much more healthy one than under a typical authoritarian headteacher. This was a small-scale attempt to implement Neill's ideas of allowing people to be involved in the decision-making which concerned their own institution.

Some staff took advantage of this type of relationship. When this happened I remembered Neill's talk in the University Staff Club. He claimed that some staff at Summerhill, unused to freedom themselves, converted it to licence and played out their own inhibitions. I was not surprised, therefore, when this happened. Staff entering a meeting via the window, feet on the staffroom tables during in-service, and some bizarre clothing were all part of this process. My way of handling this was, again, to ignore it, thereby allowing staff to play out their inhibitions, with possible beneficial results in their own relationships with the students.

When Craigie was large, we had four minibuses, which were removed from the campus by staff every night for safety. I discovered, to my horror, that one enthusiastic volunteer for this task was using the bus as a base for his black-economy window-cleaning business. This I stopped, but who knows what I would have done had he offered some of the profit to the Craigie Trust Fund?

In moments of despair we all need a bolt hole, but the option of Major Major in *Catch 22* of escaping out of the office window is not available to everyone. My basic cure was to drift around Craigie to talk to or just observe the students as they went about their daily activities. I was fortunate in that I had three places where I could recharge my batteries: the Under-Fives Centre, School House and the Resource/Learning Centre. Each had its own magic, which seemed to me to express some aspect of Neill's philosophy.

In the 1970s and early 1980s Craigie was firing on all cylinders. A child-centred Neillian type of school had been created, containing many educational innovations called the Craigie Curriculum. Visitors came from many parts of Scotland. They studied the aspect of the curriculum which interested them and left, hopefully, the wiser. Few, if any, picked up our holistic child-centred approach. Sadly, nobody worked out the importance of the Neillian connection, or even the possible contribution that the Neillian approach could make to Scottish education and to future generations of Scots.

CHAPTER TWENTY-TWO

The Future

The Tory/Thatcherite revolution has had a definite effect on education, which is, depending on one's political position, either positive or negative. It is certainly one which is not child centred. At most of the head teachers' in-service sessions that I latterly attended, children, if they were mentioned at all, were totally submerged in the world of the MBAs. The men in grey business suits had taken over. The accountants were beginning to dominate education, pushing educational theories and methodology into the background. League tables of exam results dominated discussions, as did the new methods of financing schools. No attempt was made to relate this to our growing numbers of disaffected young people.

At one such in-service session on the 5–14 Initiative, a Scottish Office Education Department-led education programme which was aimed at integrating the education of primary and the early years of secondary schooling, an HMI delivering the keynote speech stated that discussion would be permitted on all the academic subject documents but there would be no freedom of discussion on the document related to testing. I had come the full circle. This was back to the Moray House approach of uncritical acceptance I had experienced almost 40 years earlier. This time, however, I tried to open up a discussion on testing, but was ruled out of order. A generation of young Scots would grow up to be box-tickers and passers of tests. This was the old Qualifying Exam, not too cleverly disguised.

The British idea of class was returning to education with the reappearance of sump schools for the underclass, which clearly reflected the government's view of a two-tier Britain. There was to be an educational hurdle race, in which most young people would trip and fall well before the finishing line and thereby be classed as failures. Separating out the school population would again be a priority of our education system. This threat of failure can easily lead to most people wishing to finish with education at the earliest opportunity. There is a danger of treating education like a visit to the dentist, to be got over as fast as possible. This is a waste of human resources Britain can ill afford.

This drift runs counter to the philosophy of the community-school movement and the community-education service, which argues that education is a life-long process allowing people to fulfil their potential when they choose that the time is right. To re-enter the world of education is much more difficult for someone who has been constantly told, directly or indirectly, that he or she is a failure. This is, in my view, expanding Neill's vision from a child-centred education system to one that encompasses all age-groups. It becomes possible to hand people some control over their lifestyle.

My experience at Craigie made me positive that the way forward has to be one of encouragement, praise and the development of the belief that every person has something to offer society. I am convinced this is one antidote to the so-called 'yob culture'.

Instead of entering into a sterile debate about the merits and faults of comprehensive, grammar and private schools, politicians should look to the community-school movement to solve at least some of the educational problems. The development of community schools, or neighbourhood learning centres (a more acceptable title for those who have already failed under the school system), would add a new dimension to the education system and might solve some of society's current problems. Such learning centres' clients would cross the complete age spectrum. This mix could produce an additional bonus in developing inter-age tolerance, a feature sadly lacking in society. The expansion of the community-school movement is logical in a society bedevilled by unacceptable levels of unemployment. The two founders of the movement in the 1930s, Henry Morris in rural Cambridgeshire and Frank Manley in industrial Michigan, were trying to help very different types of communities ruined by massive unemployment. They developed community schools to provide people in these areas with the opportunity of either recreational or educational activities.

This development took place in the schools built with taxes, raised from the people. These schools were built for the people, by the people. This relationship is too often forgotten by the present government. Another advantage which learning centres could offer is a lack of regimentation. This could be achieved by varying the

161

characteristics of the individual centres to reflect the needs and aspirations of the communities they serve. This lack of regimentation would be another bonus for our society. There is evidence in the collective literature on community schools to suggest that recognition of local characteristics reduces the alienation which exists between the community and the local school. It was certainly true in Craigie's case.

In some respects, the opportunity may have been missed. But there are two underutilised factors that should be obvious both to society and politicians. Empty classrooms are scattered throughout the country, due to the demographic downturn of the birth-rate. The other factor is the number of unemployed trained teachers. Here is a golden opportunity to develop learning centres, in which the ideas of Morris and Manley could help to alleviate the current social problems arising from a disillusioned young population.

Often in history, the solutions to problems have already been present as dormant seeds in the society struggling to solve them. Community schools may be the seed capable of solving many of our present educational problems. For this to happen, however, requires a political party capable of recognising this opportunity, able to shake off its dogma, and pick up and nurture the community school. Who, in our society, has the foresight to use Morris and Manley's ideas to try to solve the educational problems of our present-day society?

The saddest feature for me about crystal-ball gazing is that Neill, his philosophy, and Summerhill do not feature. It is true that progress has been made. Education is more child centred and obviously less violent since the banning of corporal punishment, but his important views

162

on children, their lives and their development are difficult to find in our schools.

The current obsession that education has to be related to the 'real world', instead of the world of the child and the adolescent, needs to be rethought. Qualifications are important, but learning the skills of constructing a CV or interview techniques are being pushed lower and lower down the age-groups in schools. These are not a part of childhood. Children must be allowed their childhood. Growing up, they must have time and space to be what they are, and the adult population must allow this process to develop at its own speed. Failure to do so will only increase the alienation that already exists between the generations, with the antagonism and disillusionment which results in the violence that has become a feature of our society.

Two other important features of Neill's philosophy, namely play and pleasure, are sadly lacking in the education system of the past 17 years. Both aspects are vital if we are to raise our children in such a way that they will become happy, balanced adults. This is what education is about. If adults find this a difficult or uncomfortable concept, it is a price well worth paying if the future dividend is a more contented population. The present school population has grown up with the idealism of the free-market economy, in which the making of money, at all costs, is the aim of life. It is no accident that Dr Benjamin Spock's latest book, *A Better World for Our Children*, has been written at this point in the development of our society. The section on education is a clear plea for schools to develop in children thinking skills, problem-solving skills, skills in taking initiatives and responsibility, and, more importantly, being co-operative, creative and having

163

consideration for others. In other words, a list similar to the Craigie five Cs.

The current dilapidated state of our schools also presents a clear message to children that they are of little importance. If they were, would society not pay the cost of upgrading schools to produce a pleasant environment in which our country's future adults spend their formative years. Why not use the peace dividend in a positive way which could benefit society?

Craigie became a learning centre for the Pilton community. It tried to banish violence, develop a happy atmosphere and, in the process, produced many well-balanced individuals. When I meet former students it gives me great pleasure to talk to them. They are a credit to the Craigroyston years, the Neillian philosophy and the dedication of a superb group of professionals.

When the politician being tipped as our next prime minister comes to Edinburgh to visit his old school, Fettes College, may I suggest that he extends his visit? If he drives out of Fettes and turns west along the Ferry Road he can visit Craigie, where he will find educational ideas which will be of more use to the bulk of the population he will govern than those of his old school.

Appendix A

A PERSONAL VIEW, 1973–93

When we adults think of children there is a simple truth
which we ignore: childhood is not a preparation for life,
childhood is life. A child isn't getting ready to live, a child
is living.

Professor T. Ripaldi, *Notes on an Unhurried Journey*

Nothing in my previous life had prepared me for Craigroyston. I joined the school in 1973, having taught
English at another Edinburgh comprehensive school for
five years. I was appointed as principal teacher of guidance, and my education was about to begin.

Like many of my Craigie colleagues, I had been
nudged in the direction of the school by a golfing pal of
Hugh MacKenzie's. 'I think you'd like it there,' he smiled,
enigmatically. I made discreet enquiries. No one could

tell me anything useful except the general location of the school.

My informal visit to meet the head and see round the school brought a foretaste of the complexities to come. My first impression was that everyone, staff and students, was engaged on very urgent business and hurrying to the next important assignation. I had never experienced such a bustle of activity and directed energy in a school. At the front door, a man wearing jeans, an open-necked shirt and a large, leather CND medallion was explaining, with much expression of the arms, to two indignant parents why they should allow their troublesome teen-ager to go on an imminent school trip. At reception I asked for the headteacher. 'That's him over there,' said the receptionist, nodding at the red-haired arm waver.

My relaxed tour round the school with Hugh complete, he took me to the staffroom. Here I made my first mistake. I had just settled in a chair, anticipating a luxury free half-hour stolen from my then teaching post, when Hugh strolled in to remind me to get back to my school, fast! This apparently *laissez-faire* style and ethos of the school and its head, allied with his desire to keep us all on our toes, was to characterise the next 20 years and create the dynamic that moved us forward.

That summer term, for me, was a nightmare of meetings, the jargon and content of which belonged in an educational milieu I thought previously confined to the *Times Ed*. Real issues of what would work best for the children in our community were being addressed. Aims and objectives were drafted again and again. Like most teachers of that time, I had been guided by the 'O-grade-or-not?' principle. Suddenly, here was a school where

166

every student mattered and deserved the most appropriate education and rewards.

For the first time I encountered and gradually understood the concept of a child-centred education. Simply, we were to teach, and learn from, children, not 'mini-adults'. The absence of proscriptive school rules and regulations, apart from the global one of not harming another person, created an amazingly fertile ground for personal growth for both staff and students.

The traditional respect of the student for the teacher could not be assumed but only earned through relationships of the highest integrity. More significantly, the balance of power shifted in favour of the needs of the individual young person. There was no false barrier of authority to shelter behind when a student acted out her or his personal frustrations. Our response was to keep remembering that these were children, some of whom had no other adult listening to them.

Much of the listening, interpreting and acting on the students' behalf fell to the guidance staff, called house directors to avoid the connotations of the public-school house master and house mistress. Advocates for the students, first and foremost, they also had the almost impossible task of reconciling the needs of the students and the staff in this inventive setting. What is memorable is that we were all constantly reinventing the idea of a school which would educate all its community and not just the students who were able to 'fit in' to a blueprint.

If 'children first' was the paramount principle, parents came a close second in importance in the educational process. They were always welcome and needed no appointment system. They too had plenty to contribute. One fiery meeting between Hugh, me and a parent

167

ended with Mrs Y, in exasperation at our apparent tolerance of her daughter's shortcomings, bawling at him, 'See
you, you're nothing but a big poof!' Given the freedom
to express her feelings, she returned on the following
day, to apologise!

I felt this absence of artificial barriers of status most
keenly one day when a female student stopped me in the
corridor and ordered me to stand still. She raised her
hand and adjusted my earring. 'You were going to lose
that, Miss. It wisnae in right.' I had never before been
physically touched by a student. Twenty-two years later
I can still remember the shock of that physical contact
– which was undreamt of, impossible, in my previous
experience of schools.

This balancing act of being advocates, mentors,
friends, educators and parents to the students was made
easier by residential trips for all the students. Some staff
were 'naturals' at this; the rest of us had to learn. I was
summoned to a meeting and told that as a house director
I was expected to 'take' a field trip. I didn't even know
what a field trip was, let alone how to run one. I spent a
nervous weekend with a map of Scotland while trying to
think of any outdoor activities that I was competent in!

I remember little of that 1974 field trip: dozens of
third-year students, all wearing Bay City Rollers gear,
platform shoes compulsory, minibuses lining the drive of
the school and utter terror on my part that we were
responsible for a very *not* hand-picked bunch of 15-year-
olds. I don't think I told anyone I had never seen the
inside of a youth hostel before.

For years, most Craigroyston staff routinely
accompanied groups of students to the sunny Ratho
Centre for a three-day introduction to residential trips,

168

and many a privation we put up with. But the pay-off was huge, not only in terms of closeness between teacher and student but also between teacher and teacher. Many a confidence was offered in the course of chilly nights spent in 'shoogly' iron bunks. Characterising all of the residential experiences was the trust displayed in the staff. When students' behaviour fell short of expectations, I knew I would not be held accountable for circumstances or events that were beyond my control.

After one particularly taxing trip to the Lake District, when I had seen the inside of a couple of police stations, I was just a little jaded and doubtful about Hugh's plan to take the whole school to Europe. S1 students to the Costa Brava, all of them? The 'whole-school' vision extended to *everyone* working in the school. Clerical and administrative staff, technicians, auxiliaries and parents who had been supporting our residential trips over the years seized the opportunity to participate in the Europe trip. Teachers went to extraordinary lengths to ensure that each child could be there. One teacher achieved this for a student by standing over her parent while the passport form was signed, then processing and paying for it himself! Our friends and relatives, accustomed annually to being asked for a small donation towards trips, found themselves writing cheques for £150!

The trip was a triumph. Each day was full of play and real learning for all of us. The students guided the staff round the Dali museum at Figueras in an informed and authoritative manner, unlike some of their Spanish peers. We played on the beach like a rather large Sunday-school trip. The young people enriched the holidays of the other hotel guests, and Dutch tourists wondered at

the Scottish educational system that produced such fine
young people.

Although the emotional, physical and intellectual
demands made on the staff in this highly charged, respon-
sive school were at times almost unbearable, minor irri-
tations were swept aside. We were encouraged to take
students out of school for any valid educational reason.
Free transport was always available, thanks to the Trust
Fund. Most staff were supportive. Easy access to sympathetic, skilled clerical staff, wonderful departmental
auxiliaries, centralised, well-managed, audio-visual
equipment and freedom from the chore of getting money
from students for every trip made life much simpler.
However, it was the knowledge that we were all professionals, equally responsible and accountable for the
quality of experiences of the students, that made the
school work and often made everything seem possible.

Conflict, however, was inevitable. We were building
a curriculum and an ethos uniquely tailored to our
students' needs. As a staff, we were encouraged to be
vocal, and there was lots of shouting at staff meetings
about what the students' needs were! Often teachers
expressed that students were out of school too much,
that more time was needed in school for basic skills,
for examination syllabi, for a more authoritarian regime.
That students had complete freedom of the buildings at
break and lunchtime was a recurring discussion, always
unresolved, as the staff were never asked to give up
lunchtime to supervise the students. Very recently, I was
corrected by a student in my use of the phrase 'in my
school'. He reminded me that it was *his* school.

Parents, too, were not always convinced about the
'caring' school. I lost count of the number of parents who

stated their preference for 'the belt' to counselling. I often quaked while Hugh battled verbally with belligerent parents. One of his ploys was to 'walk away' when the situation was getting out of hand and leave the house director to sort it out!

Sometimes the conflicting needs of the students and the staff made the house director's role fairly tricky! I don't think this was or is unique to Craigie but is perhaps more marked in a truly child-centred school. With such a high profile given to 'guidance and a realistic time allocation, teaching staff not surprisingly expected a great deal of us. (I notice that when I am teaching English in the classroom, I feel the same expectation!) I did have time to spend with individual students, engaging in genuine counselling, not the 'iron-fist-in-the-velvet-glove' variety. M stands out. Together, after many hours, we discovered that she was powerless against her father's alcoholism, but if she conquered her fear of the dentist she could smile again. Years before the introduction of the term 'Youth Strategy', Craigroyston had been inventing ways of alternatively educating students for whom even our curriculum was an irrelevance. Overnight a dissident would become a vigilant and loyal 'jannie'. A young, talented but rebellious footballer was given the choice of being excluded or transferring to a nearby school whose headteacher was better placed to channel the youngster's ambitious nature. Instead of strait-jacketing students, a flexible teaching staff made it possible for us to create individual 'courses' for students built on 'favourite subjects' or 'favourite teachers'! Supported by the philosophy that all the students were our responsibility and with alternative resources like the amazing School House (still a unique establishment), we seldom experienced that 'backs-against-the-wall' feeling. Ironically, today, with 'Youth Strategy' in place, we feel less empowered.

If the students were not strait-jacketed, neither were the staff! There was never a 'dress code' although I remember a male teacher being asked by Hugh not to wear shorts, an uncharacteristic but typically complex response from him. Over the years, we seemed a very atypical staff – young (visitors always commented on this), innovative and passionate about our work and how to fuse our personal agendas into a successful school. Friday night at the pub was for fun, for being human together, for easing the high-speed pressures of the week. Occasionally, discussion led to altercation but catharsis was usually achieved. Our staff Christmas lunches became legendary. Old disputes about educational theory and practice were aired, new alliances forged, we would get 'legless' and go home for the holidays, feeling very much part of the team.

The staffroom was always full of surprises. Visitors remarked on how the staff's conversation revolved around students and not knitting patterns and the like. Occasionally, the staffroom became the setting for esoteric, theatrical games between groups of people, one involving an imaginary ship, with crew and logbook, moving slowly, silently and territorially around the room. Craigie staff were also highly entertaining in the annual pantomine put on for the students, usually with about three rehearsals and maximum silliness so that the students could roar with approval or derision at their teachers.

My early memories of Craigroyston are very vivid. Then the years rush together. I imagine this experience is shared with all my colleagues. What stands out? A seminal staff meeting where individual teachers spoke powerfully about the ineffective practice of belting, and we abolished the belt there and then; an eminent child psychologist reminding the staff that a recriminatory letter from school to home could be the final straw in a fragile family; a representative from the Region warning us of the potential pitfalls of becoming a community school. I recall vividly our initial unease at sharing the staffroom with adult students and my woeful attempts to teach adults, unlike many of my colleagues, who were highly successful with adults.

One unforgettable memory is an annual 'Womble'. Fundraising by sales of work, etc. never caught on with us. Much more attractive was to 'clean up' our community and get sponsored for doing it. In a bizarre onslaught on the area, without reference to the residents, we would lead 'the troops' into back gardens and carry back to school rubbish, furniture, litter, old TVs. 'Look what *we've* got, Miss,' said a child, pointing to a black bag. I looked. Inside was a very large, black, stinking horse's head. I think we gave up the sponsored 'Womble' quite soon after this.

I remember Tuesday nights working at the Craigie Club, a hybrid community/school youth club, so popular that hundreds of young people came to claim their territory. I would go to the pub afterwards to celebrate that the potential trouble hadn't flared up, spend Wednesdays sorting out minor hassles and on Sunday night start worrying about what might happen on the following Tuesday. After a while I decided that the other staff could manage without me!

The ultimate memory trip was the first students' reunion, in 1988. 'I remember you excluded me one day,' shrieked a young woman, 'and gave me a Mars bar.' During a television interview some years before (the school was in great demand by the media because of its progressive philosophy) I had postulated some half-baked theory about low blood-sugar levels contributing to aggressive behaviour. That night, the turnout of former students was staggering, not only in its quantity but in its variety. It was very tangible proof of what we had been working for over the years.

A recently retired member of staff had the foresight over the years to keep scrapbooks of newspaper cuttings and documents detailing events in the life of the school and the students. They contain their wedding photographs, personal tragedies, career successes and the diversity and minutiae of a school's activities, each receiving equal importance. The scrapbooks provide continuity and pleasure for our present students. I hope that the scrapbooks are being kept up to date and that we keep on responding to today's students with innovation, warmth, respect and the same desire to learn from them.

Isobel Leckie
member of staff
Craigroyston Community High School 1973–93

Appendix B

A ROOKIE'S SNAPSHOT, 1972–74

Fresh from teacher training in 1972, I was offered any one of three posts in Edinburgh and opted for Craigroyston. It was sold to me as a school with a new head, very dynamic and brimming with go-ahead ideas.

Hugh MacKenzie and I began working in Craigroyston on the same day. There were many new staff that day, embarking on their careers, eager to try new ideas and ready to be moulded. On teaching practice, many of us had been in schools where new young staff were not valued. Not so at Craigie. Within the first term we were encouraged to take on responsibilities. John Wells, another probationer, and I, both in our first year of teaching, organised a field trip to North Wales. Hugh was most supportive. He allowed us to make mistakes. We were never ridiculed and we learned from where we had gone wrong. Nowadays, young teachers have to wait so long for the kind of responsibility that Hugh was happy to give us from those very early days.

Right from that first day, I remember this character who immediately gave the impression he would be different. He was dressed differently. He made it clear he was embarking on a radical experiment, of which we were all a part.

As time wore on, his Americanisms – 'Hey, man!' – and his polo necks and flares became part of the whole picture of what was happening at Craigie. Fifty people would turn up at Friday-night pub sessions, where friendships were formed which spun off in supporting each other professionally. The pub sessions would sometimes be followed by parties at his house characterised by pints and jazz. We were young and we knew this was unusual. Perhaps we were dazzled by it. But, without doubt, it was very special, and the result of it was that we worked very hard indeed.

Sometimes Hugh made giant leaps into what seemed to us to be the dark, and they came off. CSE was very exciting. The courses were innovative. Here we were, two years out of college, writing courses and, soon after, training other teachers and moderating their work. It was unique.

Once we crossed swords. Returning from a golf trip by minibus, my driving had been less than desirable. We were hurtling home at great speed. Bags of chips flew everywhere. Hugh himself wasn't there, but by Monday morning he had heard. All he said was, 'Look, George, you're a bit of a fly boy, aren't you?'

I replied, 'OK. I won't drive so fast again.' End of incident. The attitude seemed to be that if we were working for Craigroyston we were good guys, but that did not mean we could do as we liked.

He had the ability to get us to do things which were difficult, while at the same time we were left with the impression we were doing him a favour. Early on he asked me to take a group of 12 very difficult boys out every Monday morning as part of the de-schooling programme. 'You decide what you are going to do. You're a geographer. Okay, man.' And off I went, feeling pleased to have been asked!

He was a tremendous head. He had a vision which was sculpted to meet the needs of the community. There was a sense of purpose that we were moving the school along a pre-determined path. Hugh was always meant to be a headteacher. That particular post allowed him to really develop his talents. Perhaps he wasn't such a great geography teacher – I don't know. So many people are appointed above their ability. Hugh was appointed to the level where he could shine.

I was young. I was working for a guy who had vision. The school was moving forward. It was the ideal working situation.

George Meldrum
geography teacher
Craigroyston High School, 1972–74

Appendix C

LESSONS TO LAST A LIFETIME, 1974–80

Summer 1977. It's the first week of the school holidays and there's a heatwave. It's so hot you can hear the forest crackling above the sound of the crickets. My parents and my sisters have gone to Blairgowrie for a family holiday but I'm at Lagganlia with the school.

Looking back now, it's hard to believe that after the long grind of the school year any teacher would volunteer to take a group of kids away in the first week of the holidays. These days my teacher friends spend half of May and all of June wrestling with nagging headaches and counting down the days until Trades' fortnight and a package holiday in the sun...

But back to Lagganlia. If I close my eyes and concentrate, I can still see it all so clearly. I can walk through the building from room to room, collect my packed lunch from the table in the dining-room, rush along to the kit store, pull on my boots, pack my daysack and head for the hills in a hubbub of happy voices bustling into the back of a Transit van. I can cross the loch in my canoe, claw my way up rocky cliffs, throw myself into the icy cold waters of the River Feshie, climb into my bunk and lay my head on the crisply laundered pillow, dreaming of the last-day disco and some long-lost girl.

For me, hills, rivers, tents and rock-faces were as important as the classroom. Perhaps even more so. Miles from home, we'd walk for hours, talking. We'd cook as a group, eat socially, spend the evening telling stories, singing songs and playing cards. Miles from the chalk dust, teachers were adult friends. For the first time in my life, I was on speaking terms with adults who weren't relatives or close friends of my parents. More than that, we talked and argued, and my opinion seemed to count. Gradually, I became happy to consider more and more of my teachers as friends, and once friendship has been established the classroom relationship inevitably changes.

For most children, a teacher is a kind of two-dimensional blackboard accessory who may as well be put away for the night like a rollerblind and brought out again, raring to go, in the morning. Yet Craigie teachers volunteered in alarming numbers to become real people in the lives of their students – real people with homes of their own, husbands and wives, habits bad and good, hang-ups large and small, idiosyncracies weird and wonderful and an assortment of talents which made them colourful, three-dimensional characters whose company I actively pursued.

And they cared enough to ensure that the relationship worked two ways. I recall in the first year signing up for Craigie's branch of the Young Ornithologists' Club led by biology teacher Colin Mitchell. From the start Colin and I got on pretty well, and towards the end of one school year he told me he might give me a ring during the summer holidays if he was going birdwatching.

'Yeah, right,' I thought to myself, 'sure you will.' But Colin was true to his word and made the call. I reckon it was probably the first time ever that anyone had phoned me at home (we were kind of late joining the twentieth century). Colin picked me up in his car with his wife, Pam, and we headed off to St Abbs to watch the seabirds. That kind of experience would be unusual now, never mind in the mid-1970s, but it's the kind of experience that lasts a lifetime and, to me, is of so much more value than anything you ever learn in a classroom.

Back in the classroom things were probably a bit different from the normal Scottish secondary school. Craigie was pretty informal. No uniforms, very few rules and, as my schooldays passed, gradually there was no belt. Until the belt was finally banned, it was used fairly frequently in my early years at Craigie. I've watched a teacher haul one of my classmates out for some long-forgotten misdemeanour then play a double-or-quits game of cards with the child, teasing him along with a friendly fun-filled game before reducing him to tears with one brutal blow of the belt.

Though the belt would eventually have no place in Craigie, it took some time to phase out completely so, like anyone who ever went to school, I can tell a few horror stories. Yet I like to think that my collection of negative school memories is abnormally small. Of course, stacked against the warm rosy glow which will live with me forever, there are a few bitter moments. But when they came, they probably hurt even more because Craigie's spirit of mutual trust and co-operation was so ingrained it was easy to take it for granted.

August 1979. I'm back at school for a sixth year. The holidays past have been fruitful. My exam results, though a personal disappointment, are adequate for university entrance. My plan for sixth year is simple and self-indulgent. SYS English, because that would be my degree subject, a crash course in O-grade music, because I really wanted to be a pop star, an equally compact O-grade Italian, because myself and a few others fancied learning Italian, and Higher Biology (for the first time since second year) because of the girls in that class.

It all seemed perfectly reasonable to me but first I would have to justify my course selection to a committee of worthies who had assembled in the school library to discuss courses with those staying on for a sixth year. I outlined my selection with all the obnoxious self-importance you'd expect from a teenage boy.

'What do you think you are, Renaissance Man?' joked a senior member of the Craigie staff, an old adversary who had hauled me through Higher Maths, despite my loathing of logarithms and my allergy to algebra, with a brand of fun and fear which some kids loved but, personally, I found deeply uncomfortable. My plans were shot down in flames. Higher Geography was plucked from the educational ether and presented as an instant cure for the gaps in my timetable.

I wasn't given the chance to resist. A decision had been taken. I felt cheated. I was spitting mad. Not just with the panel of suddenly distant adults, but with myself because I didn't have the confidence, the self-control or the vocabulary to argue my case.

I left the room boiling with rage, deeply wounded. I'd done my time, I'd earned a rest. But, more importantly, the Craigie spirit had been compromised. The hierarchy had been restored and my lofty idealism turned to uncomfortable embarrassment.

Years later, mellowed by reality, I look back with admiration on what I now like to see as a most cunningly crafted revenge for my failure to support the teachers' strike! I'd crossed the picket lines, like any student who saw personal preservation in the form of exam passes as much more important than the principles upon which Craigie's education system had been built. I even once brandished a two-fingered salute at a huddle of pickets which included my old friend Colin Mitchell.

But by then a new order was emerging in our society. The wave of systematic selfishness which would characterise the 1980s was already gnawing away at the egalitarian principles which had made my days at Craigie so satisfying. Thatcher's deconstruction had already begun, and the years of careful planning, the Wombling, the field trips and the welcome at the door were being undermined even before I'd finished sixth year, which, incidentally, netted me a B in Higher Geography and very little else.

Last August marked the 20th anniversary of the day I started at Craigie. Standing in the big hall in my Oxford bags and my yellow shirt with the sticky out collar, I'm waiting for my name to be called out in the class list for 1W1, waiting to embark on a six-year adventure which would provide lessons to last a lifetime.

The world has changed since then but the guiding

principles which drove the Craigie culture should be at the foundation of any school. Education is not about exams or league tables. It isn't about the three Rs, school boards or the Parents' Charter. Education is about people. It's about giving young people the opportunity to fulfil their potential with the gentle support of committed professionals whose work is more than just a way to earn a living.

Craigie cared. The certificates gather dust, the logarithms are forgotten but the values carry on. Craigie cared, and that's what counts.

Alan Munro
student
Craigroyston High School, 1974–80

Appendix D

THE CRAIGIE CURRICULUM, 1976

From 1972 to 1976 a distinctive curriculum evolved at Craigroyston High School. It was distinctive because of the following:

a. it included national certificate courses for all students of all abilities
b. the curriculum attempted to be relevant to the needs of the students
c. the curriculum attempted to widen the students' horizons
d. the curriculum attempted to compensate the students for the underprivileged environment in which they were raised
e. the curriculum was designed to include within the school the means (i.e. time and staffing) to deal with some of the current educational/social problems of the students.

These distinctive aspects of the curriculum were tackled through the media of:

a. the outdoor-education programme
b. the large-scale residential programme at Ratho and the third-year field week
c. the community-service programme
d. the eighteen CSE courses
e. the school counselling programme
f. School House.

This 1976 model continued to be upgraded over the following 16 years.

Bibliography

2. A Subversive Mess
Neill, A.S., *Hearts Not Heads in Schools*, 1945
Neill, A.S., *The Free Child*, 1953
Reich, W., *The Mass Psychology of Fascism*, 1946
Reich, W., *Listen Little Man*, 1948
Russell, B., *Why I Am Not a Christian and Other Essays!*,
    1957

3. The Liberators
Neill, A.S., *A Dominie's Log*, 1986
Neill, A.S., *Summerhill*, 1962

4. Back to Reality
MacKenzie, R.F., *State School*, 1970
MacKenzie, R.F., *The Unbowed Head*, 1980
Berg, Leila, *Risinghill: Death of a Comprehensive School*,
    1968

5. The Making of a Heidie
MacKenzie, R.F., *The Unbowed Head*, 1975

8. Rules Create Crises
MacKenzie, H.D., *Educating For Tomorrow – the Craig-royston Experience*, 1976

9. Talking the Blues Away
HMSO SED, *Guidance in Scottish Secondary Schools*, 1968

11. The CSE Road Show
MacKenzie, H.D., *Educating For Tomorrow – the Craig-royston Experience*, 1976
Williams, W.W., *Establishing and Evaluating Instructional Objectives*, 1970
MacKenzie, H.D. and Ballie, A., TESS, *CSE as a Solution to ROSLA*, 1974

15. Enter the Community – Stage Left
MacKenzie, H.D. and MacAskill, K., TESS, *A School as Part of the Local Community*, 1974
Craigroyston, *Bernard van Leer – Submissions Reports, Evaluations and Work Plans*, 1979–88

16. Enter the Little People
Watt, J., *Evaluation in Action. A Case Study of an Under-Fives Centre in Scotland*, 1988
Watt, J., *Craigroyston Community High School Under Fives – Evaluation Report*, 1986

17. Craigie Adds the Fifth C
Craigroyston, *Bernard van Leer – Submissions Reports, Evaluations and Work Plans*, 1979–88

Centre For Leisure Research, *Craigroyston and Community Schooling*, 1988

MacKenzie, H.D., *UK and USA Community Schools*, 1990

MacKenzie, H.D., *Community Education Research Digest – Accommodating Adults in High School*, 1992

18. The Heidie Goes to Court
Ross, D., *An Unlikely Anger*, 1986

19. Brochures, Budgets and Bureaucracy
Craigroyston, *Craigie 2000*, 1990

22. The Future
Spock, D.B., *A Better World For Our Children*, 1994